THE SAFFRON TALES

For Pedar Bozorg, my grandfather,
who taught me how to eat.

THE SAFFRON TALES

Recipes from the Persian Kitchen

YASMIN KHAN

Photography by SHAHRZAD DARAFSHEH *and* MATT RUSSELL

BLOOMSBURY

NEW YORK · LONDON · OXFORD · NEW DELHI · SYDNEY

BEFORE WE BEGIN, I'd like to address a sometimes perplexing question: Iran or Persia? Persia was the name given to Iran by the Ancient Greeks several thousand years ago. Since that time, the West has used the term to describe the empire and the country whose inhabitants were called Persians and who spoke the Persian language. However, people inside the country have always referred to it as Iran, a place where Iranians live, who speak their native language, Farsi.

This all changed in 1935 when the Iranian government requested that all foreign embassies refer to their country as Iran.

To Iranians, the name Iran is inseparable from their country's rich and ancient cultural traditions, which gave rise to one of the world's most influential civilizations—pioneering advances in astronomy, science, and medicine, as well as exquisite art, beautiful carpets, and architectural prowess. For most non-Iranians, however, "Iran" has no such cultural connotations and these days is more commonly associated with the country's recent political history. Because of this, some Iranians prefer to refer to their country as Persia when talking to non-Iranians, particularly when they are discussing something cultural, such as food. I use the words Iranian and Persian interchangeably in this book.

Introduction

When I was little and living in Iran, I used to sob my heart out each morning as my mother got ready to leave for work. Clinging to her legs, I would beg her not to go, and, to appease me, Mum would explain that she needed to go to work to earn money so she could buy me some pomegranates. I practically pushed her out the door when I heard this.

My obsession with pomegranates started early, nurtured by visits to my grandparents' farm where I could pick the fruit fresh from the trees. I had a knack for vigorously rubbing the leathered skin of the fruit between my hands, listening to its ruby seeds quietly pop and crunch beneath my fingers, until the pomegranate was soft and pulpy enough for me to tear a hole in one end and squeeze its scarlet juices into my mouth. I don't even want to think about the number of outfits I ruined over the years by being too hasty or clumsy in my efforts.

I was born in Croydon, south London, but my mother's side of the family comes from the sub-tropical shores of the Caspian Sea in northern Iran. Growing up in 1980s Britain, I was always acutely aware of the gulf that existed between the Iran I knew and loved and the Iran depicted on the news. As I got older, this gulf turned into a chasm and my frequent trips to Iran to visit my maternal family were greeted with surprise and intrigue from friends and colleagues alike. With raised eyebrows, people would ask probing questions, fascinated to know how an independent Western woman such as myself could take so much pleasure in visiting a country fraught with controversy and turbulence.

My answer was simple. I loved the exuberance, warm-heartedness, and affection of the Iranian people; I loved the dramatic mountains and dazzling scenery of Iran's landscapes; and I loved the garlic- and herb-infused food that harmonized sweet and sour flavors so perfectly.

Shortly after I was born, my grandparents moved to a small piece of land outside Astaneh-e Ashrafieh, a small town in the Gilan province of Iran, and began working the land, growing rice and vegetables for sale in the local markets. They grew pumpkins, squash, eggplants, tomatoes, potatoes, peppers, chiles, garlic, spinach, half a dozen different varieties of beans, and countless fresh green herbs, as well as apples, oranges, quinces, blackberries, strawberries, watermelons, cantaloupe, kiwis, greengages, persimmons, and loquat. Needless to say, no one ever went hungry at our house.

I remember sitting with my grandmother, cross-legged on the kitchen floor, making jar upon jar of pickled garlic, and being sternly lectured by my uncle, also a rice farmer, on how important it was to cook rice properly so that all the grains stayed separate. But it was my grandfather, Ahmad Rabiee, who really nurtured my love of good food. *Pedar Bozorg* (which means grandfather in Farsi) was the kind of man who would drive for several hours just to buy 2 lbs of his favorite oranges when they were in season, or embark on solo hikes through the mountainous terrain of Gilan's forests to source pots of his favorite organic honey. One time he poked me and my cousins awake with his walking stick at 6 am to share a basket of figs he'd just picked from the tree in the front garden. And we knew if we weren't up and at the table by 6:05 am, he'd have eaten the lot.

The inspiration behind this book came from my desire to share the Iran I know and love. Armed with little more than a notepad and a bottle of pomegranate molasses, I traversed almost 2,000 miles of the country's rugged landscapes searching for recipes and stories that captured modern Iranian life.

I traveled from the snowy mountains of Tabriz to the cosmopolitan cafés of Tehran, via the rice paddies of the Caspian Sea and the majestic deserts of central Iran, ending up at the tropical fishing ports of the Persian Gulf. On my journey I visited saffron farms and pomegranate orchards, artisan chocolatiers and ancient tea houses, cooking and eating with farmers, artists, electricians, and schoolteachers. As we ate together, the people I met shared the stories behind the food they love and the country they call home, and it is their stories that are interwoven with the recipes in this book.

Some of the recipes are for dishes that have been cooked the same way for thousands of years, others are modern interpretations of Iranian classics, and others still take inspiration from Persian ingredients. Many reflect my personal preference for moving toward vegetarian and plant-based food. At the heart of all of the recipes though is a common thread: a celebration of a side of Iran that never makes the headlines but that is central to its story—its amazing food.

A taste of Iran

Persian cuisine weaves together a myriad of delicate spices and elegant flavors gathered from Iran's position at the heart of the old Silk Road.

Those unfamiliar with the food often come to the *sofreh* (the patterned tablecloth on which dishes are served) expecting spicy, fiery flavors, perhaps more befitting the country's climate and politics, and are often surprised to find that the cuisine is gentle and soothing—a poetic balance of subtle flavors such as dried limes, saffron, and orange blossom.

Slow-cooked stews known as *khoresht* and elaborate rice dishes layered with herbs, vegetables, legumes, meat, nuts, and fruit are the bedrocks of Persian cuisine, creating a dazzling mosaic of scents, textures, and colors at the dining *sofreh*. There are innumerable different types of *khoresht*, with regional and seasonal specialities, but each will be sure to have a sour and sweet balance—Iran's most dominant taste.

Outside the home, kebabs are king and on every street corner you will find succulent cuts of meat or fish, often marinated with yogurt and spices, threaded onto skewers and barbecued over hot coals. Kebabs are served sprinkled with sumac (a tart red spice made from the dried berries of the sumac bush) and are either piled high on white rice or tucked into large flatbreads, and are always accompanied by some grilled tomatoes, fresh herbs, and crunchy pickles.

Iranians adore fresh fruit, which accompanies breakfast, lunch, and dinner, and those in-between times when you might want to take a break from eating. The moment you walk into an Iranian's house you will be presented with tea, sweets, and a large platter of assorted fruit, and failure to eat at least three different varieties risks causing serious offense to your host. The country's fertile soil and diverse climate nurtures peaches, apricots, grapes, persimmons, melons, kiwis, figs, cherries, quinces, and, of course, the mighty pomegranate—Iran's national fruit, shrouded in mythology and celebrated through the ages in Persian art and poetry.

Using fruit to flavor savory dishes is another defining feature of Persian food. Pomegranates, plums, greengages, sour cherries, and apricots are salted, dried, and pounded into flat fruit leathers or cooked down into pastes or molasses to be added to savory dishes such as *khoresht* and soups. When no one is looking, I've been known to sneak a teaspoon of homemade pomegranate molasses from my grandmother's fridge, relishing its pucker-your-lips sharpness. Lemon juice, pomegranate molasses, and verjuice are all used to sharpen dishes, along with the bitter and piquant juice of Seville oranges (*narenj*).

Iran is a vast country and the regional differences are striking, not only in culture, language, and climate but also in cuisine. Depending on which part of the country you are in, the dishes that are found on the *sofreh* will vary. Meatballs stuffed with prunes and walnuts might feature

in the Turkish-influenced north-east of the country. Garlicky eggplant dips might appear by the Caspian Sea. Sweet rice dishes, layered with fruit and nuts, abound in central Iran; with perhaps some spicy fried squid in the south. In each region, the *sofreh* celebrates the best local and seasonal produce, in dishes that have been perfected over centuries to suit the local climate—but there are also some nationwide commonalities.

Eating the Persian way

Traditionally the main meal of the day is eaten at lunchtime and is often a leisurely affair, followed by a short siesta. (Well, it is hot.) The *sofreh* is likely to hold a couple of larger dishes—a stew, a rice dish, or a kebab— alongside smaller plates of salads, yogurts, pickles, and platters of fresh herbs, and diners help themselves to as little or as much as they like. Meals are eaten with a fork and spoon (perfect for scooping up those mounds of steamed rice) and washed down with water, juice or *doogh*, a cool and refreshing savory drink made with yogurt and mint.

Dinner is often more casual: perhaps some bread, cheese, and herbs or simply a glass of warm milk. One of my grandfather's cherished sayings was "Eat breakfast on your own, share your lunch with your friends, and give your dinner to your enemies." This proverb encourages us to take time to quietly savor breakfast and contemplate the day ahead, take joy in our lunch and use it as a time to connect with our loved ones, and to eat lightly at night, a time when our digestive fire is at its weakest and the body is beginning to wind down for the day—a practice that is now advocated by most nutritionists.

Modernity is certainly inescapable in Iran today. It is an incredibly young country, with two thirds of the population aged under 35. This new generation of Iranians has enthusiastically embraced fast food; hamburgers, fries, and pizza are ubiquitous throughout the country. At the same time, just as in many Western countries, vegetarianism is gaining in popularity amongst Iran's middle class youth, as the social, environmental, and health implications of eating too much meat become a wider cause for concern.

Young Iranians are developing their own contemporary food culture, creatively fusing the ingredients and cooking styles of Persian and Western food. This merging of the old and the new is one of the defining features of contemporary Iranian cooking, and many of the recipes in this book reflect this, offering a selection of ancient dishes from the Persian *sofreh*, reinterpreted for the modern kitchen.

Food to feed a crowd

As with many cultures, food plays an important role in social customs and traditions in Iran. At the heart of this is the concept of sharing food, which is central to the Iranian approach to eating. An Iranian would never simply reach into the fruit bowl and take a bite of an apple; instead, they would cut the apple into slices and offer it around the whole group, even if that meant there was only one slice left for them at the end. If that happened, they would simply start again with another apple from the bowl. Sometimes when I've been traveling on my own on a bus or a plane in Iran, people sitting nearby have offered me fruit and nuts, or

some of their lunch—anything they have. Even if you have very little, it is important to share what you can, wherever you are eating, and this is one of the nation's most charming traditions.

The communal spirit cultivated through food is found in other areas of Iranian life too. On the anniversary of the death of a loved one it is customary to make vast pots of a certain dish, perhaps a soup, or a sweet saffron and cinnamon rice pudding known as *sholehzard*, and deliver portions to all of your neighbors as *nasri* (a religious and symbolic food offering).

Festive feasts

Food symbolism also features heavily at Iran's main cultural festival, *Nowruz*, the Iranian New Year. *Nowruz* is an ancient Zoroastrian celebration that marks the beginning of the Persian calendar and coincides with the spring equinox, which in the Western calendar falls on either the 20th or 21st of March. Zoroastrianism is the 2500-year-old religion of Iran, steeped in mythology and symbolism associated with the element of fire. It is believed to be one of the world's first monotheistic religions, and many of its beliefs and practices are deeply connected to nature, astronomy, and the seasons.

The weeks before *Nowruz* are all about purification rituals as the whole nation embarks on a massive spring clean, decluttering their houses and cleaning them from top to bottom. Outside of the home, a pre-*Nowruz* frenzy hits the stores and markets, which are packed from early March with people buying new goods for the New Year.

On *Char Shambe Soori*, the last Tuesday before the festival, small bonfires are lit in people's gardens or on the street. It is customary to gather with your family and jump over the flames, repeating ancient adages to cleanse yourself of any misfortune and impurities from the year before and prepare yourself for the year ahead. Symbolically, the fire takes away your yellow pallor (sickness) and feeds you its fiery red power, giving you vitality and strength for the New Year.

At the exact astronomical moment of the equinox, families gather in front of an auspicious, beautifully decorated *Nowruz* altar to see in the New Year together. This altar will always have seven symbolic objects on it, each beginning with the letter S in Farsi, representing wishes for prosperity for the year ahead.

Objects placed on the altar vary from house to house, but typically include sprouting wheatgrass symbolizing rebirth and renewal, painted eggs symbolizing fertility and creativity, candles representing life and luck, a mirror symbolizing the field of possibilities, apples representing health, garlic representing medicine, vinegar representing age and wisdom, a gold coin representing wealth, and hyacinths representing beauty. A goldfish in a bowl is always placed on the altar, symbolizing life within

life. And often the collected works of Iran's most celebrated poet, Hafez, whose work is considered to be of divine provenance, will also be on the *haft-seen* altar or, alternatively, a copy of the Quran will be featured.

Fresh herbs and greens are incorporated into many *Nowruz* dishes as they are said to symbolize rebirth and new life. The first meal of the year is *Sabzi polo baa mahi* (page 158): a mixed herb and rice dish served with fried fish (the Iranian equivalent of turkey with all the trimmings at Christmas); smaller dishes such as *Kuku-ye sabzi* (page 72), a fragrant mixed herb frittata, are popular too.

Nowruz celebrations go on for two weeks, during which time all schools and workplaces are closed as people visit friends and family, often with boxes of sweets and pastries in hand, to wish them a Happy New Year. At the culmination of the festivities, the whole country embarks on a national picnic at their local riverbank. The wheatgrass that people have been growing on their *Nowruz* altar is taken outside and they make a wish by tying knots in it. The wheatgrass is then thrown into the water and they watch it run downstream, where it will slowly merge back into the ecosystem, along with their hopes and dreams for the year ahead.

Ancient Zoroastrian teachings dominate modern Iranian culture in other ways too. The winter solstice is another significant festival in the Iranian calendar and traditionally involves Iranians staying up late into the night to commemorate the longest night of the year, feasting on red fruits such as pomegranates and watermelon, which symbolize the crimson hues of the winter sun at dawn.

The reading of poetry from Iran's most celebrated poets, such as Hafez, Khayam, Rumi, and Ferdowsi, is an essential part of the night's festivities, and many long hours are whiled away reciting poetry and nibbling on *Ajil*, a colorful mix of roasted nuts, such as pistachios, almonds, and cashews, with dried apricots, figs, and mulberries.

To this day, my parents throw *Shab-e Yalda* parties for 30 or so of their close friends, playing games that grow increasingly raucous as the night goes on. They begin the evening with high-brow Persian literature and by the early hours of the morning have descended into singing 1970s Iranian pop songs, punctuating their feasting and drinking with dancing to the rhythmic beats of hand-held *tonbak* drums.

Eating for health

Zoroastrian teachings have also had a profound effect on Iranian eating habits through their role in the development of Iran's system of traditional medicine, known as *Tebb-e Sonnati*.

Similar to Ayurveda in India and traditional Chinese medicine, *Tebb-e Sonnati* views illness as a sign that different elements within the body are out of balance and sees food and diet as important tools for bringing the body back into a state of balance and health.

Tebb-e Sonnati is a highly complex medical system whose principles are still used in everyday Iranian life. At its most basic, it categorizes food as "hot" or "cold." This has nothing to do with the actual temperature of a dish, but rather its energetic quality and the effect it has on your body when it is eaten. Every Iranian has an inbuilt encyclopedic knowledge of which foods are hot or cold, a body of knowledge largely passed on by oral tradition. When considering what to eat, an Iranian will think about which food combinations go well together, as well as what is good for their particular constitution and which foods to avoid in particular seasons or for particular ailments.

Almost all traditional Iranian recipes are based around these principles. Take *Fesenjoon*, one of the country's most popular meals: chicken poached in a sauce of ground walnuts and pomegranate molasses (page 170). Since walnuts are classified as a "hot" food, they are paired with pomegranate molasses, which is a "cold" food, in order to bring balance to the dish, and one's own body.

Traditional *Attari* shops can be found in most neighborhoods across Iran. These sell herbs, tinctures, and *arak* (distilled plant essences) and offer specific advice for physical ailments or one's personal constitution based on *Tebb-e Sonnati*'s principles. With the revival of interest in plant-based natural medicines in recent years, they have become increasingly popular.

A final note

Like many cultures around the world, Iranians welcome people to the dining *sofreh* with a blessing, our equivalent of *bon appétit*, if you will. We offer this blessing to each other when we begin and end meals, and your fellow diners will repeat it to you if you seem to be enjoying a particularly tasty meal. The phrase is *Noosh-e jan* and literally translated it means "Let your soul be nourished by what you are eating." As you journey through the tapestry of recipes in this cookbook, I wish you nothing less.

The Persian store cupboard

In 1987, my grandfather visited the UK for the first time, a five-week trip that was also his first adventure abroad. Along with wooly sweaters and presents for me and my newborn sister, he brought with him a five-kilo bag of rice, all the way from his small town in northern Iran, as he was worried that the quality of rice over here would be inferior. And that, of course, would be a disaster. Fortunately, these days a rice-toting grandfather is not essential when cooking classic Iranian food. Most of my Persian store-cupboard essentials can be bought in larger supermarkets, and the rest can be found at Middle Eastern, Turkish, or Indian grocery stores. You can also order many of these ingredients online.

Barberries
Barberries are small, red, dried berries. As they are very sharp and sour, Iranians sauté them with a little sugar and butter before adding them to dishes, where they glisten like little rubies adorning your meal.

Bread
Traditionally made in a large clay oven known as a *tanoor*, yeasted or unleavened flatbreads are eaten alongside most meals in Iran. You can find breads such as *barbari*, *sangak*, *lavaash*, or *taftoon* in specialty Iranian stores, but if they are not available then simply do as most Iranians in the diaspora do and use pita breads, wheat tortillas, Indian naan breads, or thick Turkish flatbreads to eat alongside Persian meals.

Date molasses
This dark, sticky sauce (sometimes labeled date syrup) is an incredibly versatile natural sweetener. It has a rich, treacly flavor and is useful if you want to reduce your intake of refined sugar without compromising on flavor. You can buy date molasses in any health food shop and many larger supermarkets.

Dates
Iranian dates are small, black, and so soft that they practically melt in your mouth, with a unique fudgy flavor. If you can, do check the inside of the box before buying to make sure they are fresh and soft, then keep them in the fridge so they don't dry out too quickly. If you can't find Iranian dates then I recommend using Medjool dates as they have a similar (if not quite as intense) flavor.

Dried limes
Earthy, slightly bitter, and mildly sour, dried limes are a quintessential Iranian flavoring and are central to a number of Iran's most popular stews. To cook with them, first pierce their hard shell with a fork a few times and then add whole to soups or stews so that they can rehydrate in the cooking sauces. Just before serving, squash the limes against the side

of your pot until they burst and all their juices flow into the dish. You can also grind dried limes to a fine powder in a spice grinder, for use as a seasoning, but just be aware that they can lose their intense flavor very quickly when ground, so use them sooner rather than later.

Fenugreek

Fenugreek leaf—sometimes labeled *methi* (its Indian name)—has a slightly bitter, curry-like taste. If you are new to it, add it in small pinches until the flavor is to your taste. It has an altogether different flavor from fenugreek seeds.

Golpar

Sometimes labeled "ground angelica," *golpar* is the Persian name for the ground seeds of the native *Heracleum persicum* plant, and it is used extensively in Iranian cooking. It is my favorite Iranian spice and its deeply aromatic, bitter, musky, and citrusy aroma gives many Persian dishes their distinctive flavor. As well as being added to soups, stews, and pickles, *golpar* is used to temper any sour fruit. It is commonly sprinkled on sour cherries, kiwis, or pomegranates (along with a pinch of salt) as it has the ability to accentuate a fruit's natural flavor. *Golpar* is probably the only spice in this book that you can only find in a specialist Iranian store or online, but I highly recommend trying to track it down and experimenting with it in your kitchen.

Ground rice

Ground rice is commonly used as a thickening agent, or to make pudding-like desserts, and you can find it in most Indian or Middle Eastern stores. This shouldn't be confused with rice flour, which has a completely different texture and is primarily used for baking.

Herbs

The abundant use of herbs is one of Persian cuisine's defining features, and a typical Iranian kitchen will have an assortment of jars of dried mint, dill, coriander, parsley, oregano, and fenugreek leaf in the store cupboard, and bunches of fresh basil, parsley, cilantro, chives, mint, tarragon, and dill in the fridge.

Fresh herbs are often dry fried, to evaporate some of their moisture and intensify their flavor. Because I don't always have access to large amounts of fresh herbs, I tend to stock up on dried herbs so that I can mix them half and half with fresh ones while cooking.

Indian and Asian stores are the best places to stock up on fresh and dry herbs affordably or you could try growing them at home on a window sill or in your garden.

Kashk

This pungent Iranian seasoning is made from fermented whey and has a deeply umami flavor. *Kashk* can come in liquid or dried form, which you then reconstitute with water. It has the taste of a strong goat's cheese and is used, very sparingly, as a topping for soups or alongside some dips. You can find it in Middle Eastern stores or you can use sour cream with a sprinkling of Parmesan as a substitute.

Nuts
Persians love to eat nuts plain, roasted with saffron, lemon, and salt, or ground down and cooked into stews, soups, and desserts. Almonds, walnuts, and pistachios feature in both sweet and savory dishes, bringing with them a fantastic richness, texture, and elegance.

The most important thing to remember when storing nuts is that they deteriorate when they get old and walnuts in particular can turn quite bitter, so buy them in small batches, store in airtight containers, and always taste them before using them for cooking.

Orange blossom water
This is a highly aromatic floral water made from the flowers of the Seville orange. It can vary in intensity, so use sparingly and add a little at a time until you get the balance of flavor you are comfortable with.

Pickles
Small bowls of Iranian pickles—known as *torshi*—are served with almost every meal in Iran and can range from whole bulbs of sweet and sour garlic (aged for up to 7 years), to small, salty, cucumber pickles or aromatic concoctions of spiced and diced vegetables such as eggplant, cauliflower, and cabbage. Iranian pickles are characteristically very crunchy and sour, offering a refreshing textural contrast to tender kebabs, soothing stews, and pillowy rice dishes. They are available in Middle Eastern stores or can be ordered online.

Pomegranate molasses
This is my favorite ingredient, which I add to stews, soups, and salad dressings, and dribble on ice cream. It is a thick, sticky syrup made from cooked-down, fresh pomegranate juice, and is frequently used to marinate lamb and chicken dishes in northern Iran.

As the sweetness of each batch of pomegranates will differ, it is rare to find two bottles that are exactly the same, and brands vary considerably too, so it is worth shopping around to find the one that tickles your taste buds. I like a good bit of sharpness to my molasses so always opt for Iranian brands, which tend to be quite thick. As a rule of thumb, I find Turkish varieties almost always have added sugar, which makes them quite sweet, while Arabic brands tend to be lighter in consistency, and so are better for salad dressings.

Rice
Long-grain white rice is the prized grain of Iranian cuisine, and many Iranians don't consider themselves to have eaten a proper meal without it.

I use good-quality basmati rice when I cook Iranian food because its ivory grains elongate and separate perfectly as they cook.

When it comes to making *tahdig* (page 136), the buttery, crispy rice crust that Iranians prize so highly, you will need to use a nonstick pan with a snug-fitting lid. As there are health concerns surrounding the use of nonstick pans, I recommend seeking out brands such as GreenPan, with a nontoxic coating. That said, most Iranians use rice cookers for their daily meals, as they are a quick, easy, and foolproof way to prepare rice. These are readily available online, and if you eat rice a few times a week, it is worth investing in one. Look for an Iranian rice cooker, rather than a generic Asian brand, as it will have a special feature that enables you to make *tahdig*.

Rose water

Rose water is made by simmering rose petals in barrels of water and collecting and condensing the rising steam. It has been produced in Iran for over 2,000 years and today is used not only in cooking but also therapeutically as a remedy for any number of ailments, from insect bites to headaches. As the strength varies, it is best to err on the side of caution when adding rose water to recipes as just a little bit too much of it can leave a chalky taste in your mouth. Use less rather than more until you are confident it won't be overwhelming.

Saffron

Iran is one of the largest saffron producers in the world, and there is no scent more evocative of the Iranian kitchen than saffron's sweet, earthy aroma. Iranians use saffron in a very specific way: the strands are first ground into a fine powder and then soaked in hot water, producing a highly potent, scarlet elixir that can transform a dish with just a few drops. Try to buy good-quality Iranian saffron, available in Middle Eastern stores or online, as its flavor, aroma, and color are unmatched.

Sour cherries

Sour cherries are very popular in Iran, where they are eaten fresh or made into juice, jam, fruit tarts, and even layered into rice dishes. While you can sometimes find whole frozen sour cherries, or even very tart Iranian ones that need rehydrating in water in some Middle Eastern stores, for the recipes in this book I recommend using the packets of dried sour cherries (sometimes labeled Morello cherries) that are sold in larger supermarkets or health food shops, and are often lightly sweetened with fruit juice.

Sumac

This tangy, lemony spice is made from the dried and ground berry of the sumac bush and provides a fantastic acidic kick to any dish. In Iran it is always served alongside fish, chicken, or lamb kebabs, but I also love it as a final flourish on a salad to add a dash of color or an extra bit of zing.

Tamarind

Tamarind is a chewy sweet-and-sour fruit that is very popular in southern Iranian cooking, where its pulp is added to stews and soups, giving a characteristically tart flavor. I like to buy blocks of tamarind pulp to use in my cooking. You need to first soak it in hot water to soften it and then run the pulp through a sieve to remove the stones. Tamarind paste is also widely available and can be used in any of the recipes that follow, but do be aware that the pastes are often preserved with salt, sugar, or other additives which will affect the taste of your final dish, so you may have to adjust the seasoning.

Yogurt

As well as being an excellent digestive aid, yogurt adds a welcome cooling element according to *Tebb-e Sonnati* (Iran's traditional medicine system; see page 19) and is essential to counterbalance the richness of some Iranian stews. It is served with every meal in Iran, either in its natural state or mixed with vegetables for a more substantial side dish. Keep a big pot of natural yogurt in the fridge and use it liberally alongside any Iranian dishes—it has a particular affinity with the rice-based ones.

USING THE RECIPES IN THIS BOOK

Cooking in Iran rarely involves following a recipe. Measurements are always approximations, grabbed in handfuls and pinches, and ingredients are always comfortably substituted with whatever is available in the shops that day. Persian cooking is informal, unpretentious, and relaxed. A little bit more of this or less of that won't make any difference to most of the dishes in this book, and I encourage you to use these recipes as a guide rather than a prescriptive set of instructions. (Although it's worth noting that the oven temperatures are for conventional ovens; if you are using a convection oven, simply reduce the temperature by about 25°F.)

Do as the Iranians do and use your taste buds and your eyes to determine which direction a dish should go in. Taste your dishes throughout the cooking process so you get a feel for the dish. Remember that you can always add but you can't take away, so add your ingredients in stages and know that the final third of cooking time is when you can make the most useful tweaks to a dish. A dash of olive oil here, a squeeze of lemon there, or a generous sprinkling of salt is sometimes all that is needed to elevate an average-tasting dish to an exceptional one.

So season well, use whatever oils you prefer, substitute herbs if you need to, and, above all, just enjoy the process of cooking something new.

BREAKFAST

MANY IRANIANS WILL tell you that breakfast is their favorite meal of the day. No matter how early people have to get up—and Iran is a nation of pre-dawn risers—taking time to enjoy the first meal of the day is considered essential.

The delight of a Persian breakfast lies in the variety of different flavors you can put together for each bite. Breakfast will always include toasted flatbread, salty feta, and creamy butter, washed down with small glasses of sweet black tea. There may be homemade jams made from local fruit such as quinces, figs, blackberries, and sour cherries, as well as honey, fresh dates, tahini, and perhaps, if you are in luck, a slab of thick, wobbly whipped heavy cream or crème fraîche.

Walnuts and almonds, soaked in water overnight to make them easier to digest, are offered in little bowls alongside platters of fresh herbs and thin slices of tomato and cucumber for those who prefer a savory start to the day. Eggs are boiled, fried, or whisked into an omelette for those who want something more substantial. As ever in Iran, a bowl of seasonal fruit will always be nearby to end the meal.

This chapter features a mix of sweet and savory Persian-inspired breakfasts for everything from a grab-and-go morning snack to a hearty weekend brunch.

Persian ajil granola

Iranians nibble on ajil —a colorful mix of dried fruit, nuts, and seeds— throughout the day. This recipe incorporates one of my favorite combinations into a classic granola, which is quick and easy to make and so much better for you than the sugar-laden shop-bought stuff.

The key to getting nice crunchy chunks of granola is to use large, uncut jumbo oats and not to over-stir the mixture either while it is cooking or before it is completely cool.

This will keep in an airtight container for about 2 weeks, and is delicious served with yogurt and fresh fruit or simply with some cold milk.

3 tbsp sunflower oil
²/₃ cup date molasses (or substitute maple syrup)
2 tbsp honey
¾ tsp vanilla extract
3 cups jumbo rolled oats
A large pinch of sea salt
3 tbsp sunflower seeds

3 tbsp pumpkin seeds
¼ cup pistachios, roughly chopped
⅓ cup sliced almonds
¼ cup mixed, dried fruit, such as sour cherries, raisins, apricots, mulberries, and figs, roughly chopped (optional)

Pre-heat the oven to 325°F.

Drizzle the sunflower oil, date molasses, honey, and vanilla extract into a small bowl and stir well.

Mix the dry ingredients, except the almonds and fruit, in a large bowl, then pour in the sticky mixture and stir well to coat everything.

Tip the mixture onto two large baking trays and pat down with a wooden spoon. Place the trays in the pre-heated oven and cook for 12 minutes. If you are using two oven shelves then remember that the top one will cook the granola quicker so keep an eye on it to make sure it doesn't burn.

Take the trays out of the oven, add the flaked almonds and gently stir. Return to the oven for a final 10–15 minutes until the granola is evenly toasted. Keep a close eye on the granola as it can quickly burn.

Leave to cool on the tray, then stir in the dried fruit. Store in an airtight container for up to 2 weeks.

Makes 1 large jar

Date, almond, and tahini energy balls

Bandar Abbas is a large bustling port town in the south of Iran, and is famous for its dates and tahini, which are sensational for breakfast wrapped up in fresh, hot naan bread. I am now addicted to this delicious food pairing and devised these healthy energy balls as a quick and easy breakfast on the go. You can whizz these up in a food processor in seconds and, trust me, you'll never want to spend money on expensive energy bars again. They will keep in an airtight container in the fridge for about 2 weeks and also freeze well, so you can make a big batch and keep coming back to them.

1 cup whole almonds, plus
    2 tbsp ground almonds
³⁄₄ cup Iranian or Medjool dates, pitted

2 tbsp tahini
¹⁄₄ tsp ground cinnamon
¹⁄₄ tsp vanilla extract
A pinch of sea salt

Place all the ingredients, apart from the ground almonds, in a food processor and blitz until everything comes together into a ball—you want the mixture reasonably smooth but with a few grains of almond still visible for texture.

Roll the mixture into 16 small balls, around 1 inch in diameter. Have a bowl of water nearby to dip your hands into, as the mixture will stick to your hands.

Spread the ground almonds onto a large plate and roll each ball around in the nuts to get a fine, even coating.

Place the energy balls in an airtight container and chill for at least 1 hour before serving.

Makes 16 balls

Date and cinnamon omelette
Gheysavah

I first ate this dish on a chilly February morning at the home of Maman Betty, a lovable grandmother from Tabriz who sat me in her kitchen and fed me plate after plate of local delicacies until I could barely speak. Tabriz is a city in the mountainous north-west of Iran, where winter temperatures rarely reach more than 2 or 3 degrees above freezing in the daytime and where the local food is hearty and filling. This sweet omelette, filled with dried fruit and warming spices, is incredibly soothing on a weekend morning, when all you want to do is snuggle up on the sofa with the newspapers. As the dark, sticky dates begin to caramelize in the cinnamon- and ginger-flavored butter, they will fill your kitchen with a deliciously cozy, sweet scent—a rather fine way to start the day, I'm sure you'll agree.

¹/₄ cup pitted Iranian or
    Medjool dates, halved
A couple of pinches of cinnamon
A small pinch of ground ginger
3 tbsp cold water

2 eggs
A pinch of sea salt
2 tsp milk
Scant tbsp butter

Place the dates, a pinch of cinnamon, the ground ginger, and water in a small pan. Stir well, put a lid on the pan, and cook on a low heat for 5 minutes, until the dates have softened.

Meanwhile, crack the eggs into a bowl with a pinch of salt and the milk. Beat with a fork until fluffy.

Put a frying pan over a low heat and let it get hot. Add the knob of butter. When the butter has melted and is bubbling, add the dates and fry for 2 minutes. Space the dates out evenly in the pan and then pour the eggs in, giving the pan a gentle shake to spread them out evenly.

Cook until the omelette is almost set and then fold in half and lightly press down. Slide onto a plate and dust with cinnamon just before serving.

Serves 1

Tomato and spring onion omelette
Omelette-e gojeh farangi

Variations of this delicious tomato and turmeric-spiced omelette are eaten for breakfast all over Iran. Tomatoes are so popular in the modern cuisine, it is easy to forget that they are relatively new to Iran and only started being cultivated there from the nineteenth century. Their name in Farsi means "foreign plum"—something I've always found charmingly exotic for such an everyday ingredient. The ripeness of the tomato will determine how tasty this dish is, so buy the plumpest and deepest red tomatoes you can find and keep them out of the fridge, as chilled tomatoes lose so much of their flavor and aroma.

1 large tomato
2 eggs
A generous pinch of turmeric
Sea salt and black pepper
2 tbsp light olive oil

2 spring onions, trimmed and finely chopped
1 tbsp chopped cilantro, to garnish

Start by skinning your tomato. Bring a kettle of water to the boil. Use a sharp knife to score a small cross into the base and top of the tomato. Place in a bowl, cover with the boiling water, and leave for a minute or two. Remove with a slotted spoon and rub the skin off. If the skin doesn't come off easily then leave it for another minute. Slice the tomato in half, spoon out the seeds and discard them, then roughly chop the flesh into chunks.

Crack the eggs into a small bowl and season with turmeric, salt, and pepper.

Heat a frying pan on a medium heat, then add the oil and swirl it around. Add the spring onions and fry until they are soft. Carefully add the chopped tomato, standing back from the pan as it might spit as it cooks. Season with a touch of salt and pepper and then cook until the tomatoes are soft and most of their liquid has gone.

Pour the eggs into the frying pan, let them just set, and then gently stir a couple of times, rubbing the bottom of the pan with a wooden spoon to allow the bits of runny egg on top of the omelette to travel to the bottom of the pan.

When the omelette is almost cooked, fold the two edges into the middle. Slide onto a plate and finish with a sprinkle of fresh cilantro.

Serves 1

Baked eggs with spinach and sumac
Nargissi esfinaj

In Farsi, this simple yet elegant breakfast is named after the narcissus flower ("nargissi"), as the baked eggs in the center of the dish resemble the white and yellow petals of its spring bud.

Spinach is native to Iran and the English word for it comes from the Farsi, "esfinaj."

In place of the traditional sharp and slightly bitter taste of "narenj" (the juice of Seville oranges), I use a combination of fresh orange and lime juice here, which works just as well with the earthy leaves. I like to bake the eggs in individual ramekins, but you could also cook everything in a small baking pan or an ovenproof frying pan.

1½ tbsp butter
1 tbsp sunflower oil
½ onion, finely chopped
Sea salt and black pepper
1 garlic clove, crushed
9 oz spinach

1 tbsp fresh orange juice
1 tsp lime juice
4 eggs
1 tsp sumac, to garnish
Toasted flatbread, to serve

Pre-heat the oven to 400°F. Melt the butter with the sunflower oil in a large frying pan. Add the onion, sprinkle with ½ teaspoon of salt, and fry over a medium heat for 10 minutes. Add the garlic and cook for a further 2 minutes, then set aside.

Place the spinach in a large saucepan, season with a pinch of salt and pepper, and cook for a few minutes until the spinach has just wilted. Drain in a colander, leave to cool slightly, and then squeeze out the excess water with your hands. Roughly chop and add it to your onions, along with the orange juice and lime juice.

Divide the onion-spinach mixture between four small ramekins. Make a small well into the center of each and crack in an egg.

Place the ramekins on a baking tray and cook in the oven for around 12–15 minutes, depending on how you like your eggs. Garnish with the sumac and serve with some warm, toasted flatbread.

Serves 2

Scrambled eggs with feta and dill

Panir bereshte

This regional speciality from the northern province of Gilan brings together fragrant, sweet dill with creamy, salty feta in a perfect weekend breakfast or light lunch dish, served with warm toasted bread. This is one of those simple recipes that every Gilaki student learns how to cook as soon as they leave home, since it uses store-cupboard ingredients and comes together in minutes. The trick to making good scrambled eggs is to avoid overcooking them, so they remain fluffy and moist. I find the best way to do this is to take them off the heat when they are ever so slightly underdone and let them finish cooking in the heat of the pan.

4 eggs
Sea salt and black pepper
1 tbsp sunflower oil
Scant tbsp butter
$^1/_2$ cup (2 oz) feta, roughly crumbled into chunks

$^1/_2$ tsp turmeric
2 tsp dried dill
Toasted bread, to serve

Crack the eggs into a bowl, gently beat them with a fork and lightly season with salt and pepper.

Place a small frying pan over a low heat for about a minute before adding the oil and butter. (Heating the pan first reduces the chances of your eggs sticking later.) When the butter has melted, add the feta and cook for about 20 seconds until the cheese begins to melt and ooze.

Pour the beaten eggs into the pan, then scatter over the turmeric and dill. Leave to cook for 20 seconds without stirring, then lightly fold the ingredients together to ensure an even mix. Leave to cook for a further 15 seconds before folding the mixture together again.

Continue like this, folding occasionally but not continuously, until the eggs are almost cooked but still a bit runny. At this point, remove from the stovetop and let the eggs finish cooking for 1 minute in the heat of the pan. Serve at once, with warm toasted bread on the side.

Serves 2

Saffron and cardamom vermicelli with fried egg
Baalaaloot

When you are in need of some soul food, rustle up this indulgent breakfast of sweet, buttery noodles topped with a fried egg. I first sampled this dish in Bandar Abbas, in southern Iran, when student Aida Jafari took me for breakfast at a bustling local café. Like much of the food from this region, it takes its inspiration from the Indian subcontinent—in this case, "saviyan," a dessert made from whole-wheat vermicelli—before being given a Persian twist. This is good with or without the fried egg, but just be sure to eat it immediately for the best flavor.

4 cardamom pods
A pinch of saffron strands
3 tbsp superfine sugar, plus an extra pinch
2 tbsp freshly boiled water
Sea salt
1½ tbsp butter or coconut oil
5 oz vermicelli nests (made with durum wheat)
2 eggs

To garnish:
1 tbsp sliced almonds, toasted
1 tbsp roughly chopped pistachios, toasted

Place the cardamom pods in a mortar and work with a pestle to get the seeds out of the pods. Discard the pods and grind the seeds to a fine powder. Transfer to a small bowl.

Make a saffron liquid by grinding the saffron strands with a pinch of sugar using the pestle and mortar and then adding 2 tablespoons of boiling water. Leave to steep.

Bring a large saucepan of water to the boil with 1 teaspoon of salt and ¼ tablespoon of the butter or a dash of the coconut oil. Add the vermicelli and cook for 3–4 minutes until al dente. Stir the vermicelli while it is cooking so the strands don't stick together. Drain and rinse in cold water.

Return your saucepan to a very low heat and tip in the rest of the butter or oil, the 3 tablespoons of superfine sugar, the saffron liquid, and the ground cardamom. Cook for a few minutes until the fat and sugar have melted.

Place the cooked vermicelli back in the pan and turn the heat up to medium high. Stir to coat the vermicelli in the sauce and cook until all the liquid has evaporated and the vermicelli is quite dry.

Place a lid on the pan to keep it warm and fry your eggs with a sprinkling of salt, to contrast with the sweetness of the noodles.

Serve the vermicelli in bowls with the fried egg on top, scattered with the toasted nuts.

Serves 2

Spiced pumpkin preserve
Morab-ye kadoo halvaa-ee

Based on a popular Iranian jam made with pieces of candied butternut squash, this is a thick, lightly spiced preserve that tastes somewhat like the filling of a sweet pumpkin pie. It is amazingly versatile and can be enjoyed slathered on buttery toast, spooned into bowls of natural yogurt, or dolloped on top of a cheesecake or meringues. My recipe works just as well with any kind of pumpkin or sweet winter squash, so use whatever looks good. And make it in small batches—it has less sugar than most homemade jams, so needs to be stored in the fridge and eaten within a month.

(pictured top left on page 44)

One $1^{1}/_{2}$ lb pumpkin, peeled and seeds removed
$1^{2}/_{3}$ cups water
$1^{1}/_{4}$ cups granulated sugar
3 tbsp honey
$1^{1}/_{2}$ tsp ground cinnamon
1 tsp ground ginger
6 cloves, ground
A generous pinch of nutmeg
A pinch of sea salt
1 tbsp lemon juice

Cut the pumpkin into $^{3}/_{4}$-inch cubes, place in a large saucepan and cover with $1^{2}/_{3}$ cups water. Put the lid on the saucepan and cook over a medium heat for 12–15 minutes, until the pumpkin is soft. Blend the mixture until you have a smooth purée.

Add the sugar, honey, spices, a pinch of salt, and the lemon juice and cook for 10 minutes over a medium heat. Partially cover the pot with the lid for the first 5 minutes of cooking. When the mixture starts to spit, give it a stir, then put the lid on fully and turn the heat down low for the remaining 5 minutes.

Pre-heat the oven to 275°F and, while the pumpkin is cooking, sterilize two 13-ounce jam jars. Wash the jars and their lids in hot soapy water and place in the hot oven for about 10 minutes (lids not on the jars). When they are completely dry, remove from the oven.

When the preserve has cooked down to a thick consistency, pour into the sterilized jars and seal. Store in the fridge as soon as the jars have cooled, and eat within a month.

Makes 2 x 13-ounce jars (3 cups)

Carrot, cardamom, and rose water jam

I have a real soft spot for floral Persian jams. There is something about having cardamom and rose water at the first meal of the day that feels invitingly sophisticated. Plus, anything that acts as an excuse for me to consume more bread and butter is never a bad thing in my book. As carrots don't have a lot of the natural setting agent pectin, don't expect a firm set: this is more of a syrupy preserve. For a sweet and savory twist, try pairing the jam with some feta or ricotta.

4 cardamom pods
Zest of ½ orange
2 cups water
1¼ cups granulated sugar

3 large carrots, peeled and grated
1 tbsp lemon juice
1 tbsp rose water

Place the cardamom pods in a mortar and work with a pestle to get the seeds out of the pods. Grind the seeds to a fine powder, then place the seeds and the pods in a large pot along with the orange zest, water, and sugar. Bring to the boil and then turn down the heat and simmer for 10 minutes.

Add the grated carrot and boil for 20 minutes, until the carrot is soft and the water it is cooking in is syrupy.

Pre-heat the oven to 275°F and, while the carrot is cooking, sterilize two 13-ounce jam jars. Wash the jars and their lids in hot soapy water and place in the hot oven for about 10 minutes (lids not on the jars). When they are completely dry, remove from the oven.

Once the carrot has been cooking for 20 minutes, stir through the lemon juice and rose water and cook for a further 5 minutes.

Remove from the heat, pour into the sterilized jars, and seal. It is fine to leave the cardamom pods in the jam, as they will continue to give it flavor—just remember to remove them before eating.

When the jars are cool, store in the fridge, and eat the jam within a month.

Makes 2 x 13-ounce jars (3 cups)

RASHT
*Tales of rice paddies
and tea plantations*

The lush green countryside surrounding Rasht, the capital of the Gilan province in northern Iran, provides a scenic backdrop for sampling some of the country's most enticing food. Its soaring mountains, dense forests, and trickling streams are interwoven with rice paddies, tea plantations, and olive groves that flourish in the region's fertile, sub-tropical climate.

My family has its roots in Gilan, and it was here that as a child I spent long, balmy summer holidays running around my grandparents' farm with my cousins. Under the hot sun, we would scamper through rice paddies, jumping in and out of water pools to cool off and resting under the shade of the fig, apple, and greengage plum trees. Each year, countless clothes were ruined following the discovery of a new thicket of blackberries, and new muscles were flexed carrying watermelons the length of our forearms to the nearby stream for picnics.

The cuisine of Gilan is as green as its landscape. Mounds of fresh cilantro, parsley, and dill are cooked down to create fragrant bases for stews and *kukus*. Garlic is invited to every meal, either simmered by the bulb in sauces, pickled in vinegar, or plucked of its sprouting leaves, which are sautéed with split peas. Often we would eat fresh young garlic raw, delicately unwrapping cloves at the table and nibbling on them as we tucked into our *khoresht*.

Eggplants, squash, and pulses make up the bulk of traditional Gilaki food, making this the best place in Iran for vegetarians. It is also home to one of the country's most majestic food pairings, ground walnuts and pomegranate molasses, which come together in an earthy, sweet and sour paste used to marinate kebabs, stuff fish, or poach chicken.

Each spring the heavily scented flowers of Seville oranges are distilled to make orange blossom water, which is added to jams, rice dishes, and pastries. Orange blossoms are also dried and sprinkled into the loose-leaf tea from Lahijan, in the south of the region: this was the first place in Iran to cultivate tea. Lahijan tea is delicate and light and Iranians drink endless rounds of it, always black, always served in small, clear glasses.

In the city of Rasht, I spent an afternoon cooking with Sima Mohamadzahdeh, a pharmacist who had offered to teach me how to make *Aloo esfinaj*—a plump chicken, spinach, and prune stew (page 169). As she put me to work, searing the chicken in a large pan of sizzling hot oil, I asked her what she thought it was that makes Gilan cuisine distinctive. "Food is more garlic-based here than in the rest of Iran," she tells me, "and being so close to the sea, we always like to have a bit of fish with every meal—smoked, salted, or fried."

This rings true for me. We always had some smoked fish roe (*ashpal*) or crispy fried river fish (*kuhli*) alongside meals at my grandparents' house. On occasion we'd even enjoy some local caviar, back in the days before over-fishing took its toll. I loved eating the small, black, salty eggs with bread and butter for breakfast. Sturgeon, the fish that produces caviar, is also used to make succulent kebabs in Gilan, doused in a simple dressing of Seville orange juice and extra-virgin olive oil.

With all this exceptional produce around, it is no surprise that the people of Gilan are known throughout Iran for being *shekamoo*, the Farsi word for people who love food and eat plenty of it. "Iranians spend a lot of time eating," Sima points out. "I just got back from visiting my sister

in Canada. For lunch, she takes just a small piece of chicken and some salad to work with her and eats at her desk. In Iran, we put aside a few hours to eat our lunch. I close my pharmacy at 1 pm and come home for a proper meal with the family." She laughs. "Then of course we all enjoy a little siesta."

Eating this way has its roots in the region's historic farming traditions. To find out more about the agrarian way of life, I spent some time with Roya Baighi, a farmer from Astaneh-e Ashrafieh, a small town in central Gilan. Roya studied agriculture at college, but her studies were cut short in 1979, when the Islamic Revolution led to universities being closed for a few years. After getting married, she moved in with her husband's family and threw herself into farming life.

"I harvested rice and beans and vegetables like eggplant and corn," Roya recalls. "You have to work from dawn till dusk, especially in the summer, but I love the life and I get energy from seeing my plants grow. I still coo over purple eggplant flowers as if they're my children!" Showing me around her farm, Roya pauses to collect handfuls of fresh green leaves for the lunch we will prepare together: a Gilaki herb stew (page 152). "We try to grow as much as we can organically and live off that," she explains. "That way, we can avoid the pesticides and chemicals of the fruit and vegetables in the market—and of course it tastes so much better too."

To discover what keeps Gilaki workers going all day, I met with Babak Rabiee, a young electrician who is also from Astaneh. Warm and charismatic, Babak has an infectious grin and a mischievous twinkle in his eye, as if he is always on the brink of doing something he probably

shouldn't. At a roadside café, we breakfasted on *kaleh parcheh*, a broth made from the meat and bones of a lamb's head, along with a portion of tongue and cheek. Not a breakfast for the faint-hearted. Some freshly baked flatbread and halved Seville oranges completed the meal, and Babak showed me how to squeeze the juices into the broth.

Babak was in his final year of university and, like many people at this stage of life, was trying to decide what to do next. "I'm not sure yet. I might continue my studies and do a Master's, otherwise I'll have to do military service." Completing two years of military service within Iran is compulsory for men after they finish their formal education. In addition to the usual uncertainty about what that might entail, and about being posted far from friends and family, Babak had serious concerns—what with him being a typical Gilaki *shekamoo*. "One of my friends told me that his sergeant made their unit throw their lunches on the floor and then walk over the food in their army boots. Then he made them eat it, all of it, right off the floor!"

No sooner had I laid my spoon down in my empty bowl and wiped the corners of my mouth with my now greasy napkin than Babak insisted we try another breakfast spot. We waddled across the road to a café serving *Loobia pokhte* (page 70), a rustic dish of beans infused with citrus and golpar, served with a fried egg, tomatoes, cucumber, and flatbread.

Mid-feast, Babak patted his belly: "I love that feeling you get when you are eating something really tasty and can't stop, even though you are full." I told him that the Georgians have a word for that—*shemomedjamo*, which is not too dissimilar to the Farsi word for a person who eats too much. And I reached for another piece of bread...

MEZZE & SIDES

TRADITIONALLY, PERSIAN FOOD doesn't separate starters from main courses. Instead, the table or *sofreh* is dotted with small plates of vegetables, yogurt, olives, pickles, and salads that are eaten alongside the rice dishes, stews, and kebabs.

This chapter celebrates that tantalizing array of small plates, many of which will be recognizable as Iranian interpretations of classic Middle Eastern dishes, including burnt eggplant dips, yogurts flavored with vegetables and herbs, and, of course, falafel, the ubiquitous street-food snack that is popular throughout the region.

There is also a selection of recipes that can be served as lighter meals, or as starters, such as *kuku*, a type of frittata that is many an Iranian's standby dinner, as well as a common sandwich filling. A *kuku* is a fantastic way to use up a glut of seasonal vegetables and, paired with some salad and bread, makes a delicious light lunch or dinner.

Stuffed into pockets of bread, the *kuku* is standard picnic food in Iran, where it is often taken along on hikes to enjoy amidst the lush mountains and forests. My aunt would always make a big batch whenever we headed out on family trips to Gilan's waterfalls on our summer holidays. My cousins and I would stampede into the first crisp, cool stream we spotted, emerging tired, cold, and hungry, ready to devour her hearty herb and potato *kuku*, adding thick slices of tomato, cucumber, and sour pickles to our wraps before collapsing drowsily under the shade of the trees.

Mixed herb platter
Sabzi khordan

This is less of a recipe and more of an introduction to one of the cornerstones of Persian cuisine—eating fresh herbs with every meal.

"Sabzi khordan" literally means "eating greens." A platter of fresh seasonal leaves is placed in the center of the dining table in Iran for each person to help themselves, alongside their plate of food. As well as being high in nutrients and great for your digestive system, herbs are also fantastic for the palate, offering a fresh, cleansing, and bright contrast to some of the heartier Iranian main course stews and rice dishes.

The list of ingredients here should be used as a guide only—you can include whatever green herbs you like. Just try to have a mix of at least four different types, along with something crunchy like radishes or spring onions. If you like, add some walnuts and feta for a refreshing starter to serve with flatbread.

1 small bunch chives
1 small bunch basil
1 small bunch mint
1 small bunch tarragon
1 small bunch parsley

1 small bunch cilantro
6 spring onions, trimmed
and quartered
A handful of radishes, halved
or left whole

Wash the herbs and dry in a colander lined with paper towels or use a salad spinner to remove any excess water.

Snip off the dried-up ends of the chives. Trim away any rough edges on the rest of the herbs, but leave the stalks on. Arrange on a platter or serving plate, then add the spring onions and radishes at the side.

Take to the table and encourage everyone to help themselves.

Serves 4

Olives marinated with walnuts and pomegranates
Zaytoon parvardeh

The olive groves of Ramsar in northern Iran provide the region with an abundance of rich, nutty, and intensely flavorsome oil and fruit. This popular appetizer showcases the local produce by combining green olives with a tangy sauce made from ground walnuts, herbs, and pomegranate molasses.

Olives cured in oil are the best to use here, but if you can only find olives in brine then soak them in a couple of changes of water for an hour to get rid of their saltiness, then add an extra spoonful of olive oil to the mix. Try to use the freshest walnuts you can, as old walnuts leave a slightly bitter aftertaste.

Serve the olives in small bowls alongside a main meal of Gilaki food—such as the Garlicky beans with dill and egg (page 151) or Gilaki herb stew (page 152)—or as part of a mezze of small dishes to start a meal.

$^1/_4$ cup walnuts
2 cups oil-cured green olives, drained and pitted
1 tbsp extra-virgin olive oil
1 tbsp pomegranate molasses
$^1/_4$ tsp dried mint
3 basil leaves, finely chopped
$^1/_2$ garlic clove, minced
A generous pinch of golpar (optional)
Sea salt and black pepper
A handful of pomegranate seeds, to garnish

Grind the walnuts to a fine powder with a pestle and mortar or a spice grinder. Place them in a medium-sized bowl with the olives, olive oil, pomegranate molasses, mint, basil, garlic, and golpar (if you are using it). Season with a generous pinch of salt and some freshly ground black pepper.

Mix well, then taste and adjust the seasoning. If you think you'd like the dish sharper, add a touch more pomegranate molasses.

Leave to marinate for at least an hour and sprinkle with the pomegranate seeds just before serving. These olives keep well for several days in the fridge.

Serves 6–8, as part of a mezze

Easy naan bread

Iranian flatbreads are some of the oldest in the world, their popularity spreading across the Levant and into India, where the locals adopted the Farsi word for bread, "naan." There are bakeries on every street corner in Iran and people buy freshly baked breads daily to eat with every meal. The most popular kinds are yeasted flatbreads such as naan-e barbari or naan-e sangak, which are baked in a tanoor (a traditional clay oven) in huge pieces, up to 3 feet long. They are tantalizingly soft and fluffy on the inside, with a firm crust. Cooking the bread in a frying pan is a quick and easy variation to try at home. If you have never made bread before, then this is a great place to start.

1 1/2 tsp fast-action dried yeast
1 tsp superfine sugar
1/2 cup lukewarm water
2 cups strong white bread flour,
   plus extra for dusting

1 1/2 tsp sea salt
1 tbsp light olive oil or sunflower oil
1/4 cup natural yogurt

Place the yeast, sugar, and 2 tablespoons of the lukewarm water in a glass and stir well. Leave to sit for 5 minutes.

Place the flour and salt in a large mixing bowl. Make a well in the middle. Pour the oil and the yogurt into this well, along with the yeast mixture. Then slowly pour in the rest of the water and mix with your hands. The dough should feel very sticky, so if it seems too dry or stiff, add a touch more water.

Tip the dough out on a lightly floured surface and knead for 5 minutes: use the heel of your palm to repeatedly push down on the dough and fold it in on itself until it can easily be shaped into a smooth ball. Place the dough in a bowl, cover with a damp tea towel, and leave to rise in a warm spot for 1 1/2 hours.

Tip the dough back out onto the lightly floured surface and knock it back to get rid of the air bubbles: fold the bread in on itself using the heels of your palms for a few minutes, until it is smooth and all the air has been pushed out.

Divide the dough into six even-sized balls. Meanwhile, place a 9-inch-wide frying pan over a medium heat to warm up.

Take a ball, flatten it into a small round disc with your fingers and dust each side with a little flour. Use a rolling pin to roll it out until it's nearly as big as your frying pan and around 1/8-inch thick. Dust your rolling pin with a little flour if it begins to stick.

Pick the dough up from one end and hang it for a few seconds to stretch it slightly into an oval shape. Cook it in the hot pan for about a minute until it starts to bubble. Turn it over and cook the other side for a minute. Repeat until the bread is toasted to your preference and there are no soft doughy bits. This can take 4–6 minutes total cooking time, depending on how toasty you like your bread.

Once cooked, cover the bread with a clean tea towel to keep it warm while you make your other naans.

Makes 6 naan breads

Persian flatbread
Lavaash

Lavaash is a very thin, unleavened flatbread, which has been made in the Middle East for thousands of years, and can be bought in any Iranian or Middle Eastern store. It is traditionally baked in a tanoor and then left to dry. Treated in this way, it can be stored for up to a year and rehydrated with a sprinkle of water before serving. This recipe gives you as close an approximation as you can get without a clay oven, by cooking the bread in a dry frying pan. Although lavaash is usually made with white flour, I like to add some whole wheat flour for flavor and texture.

These flatbreads can be served as an accompaniment to any meal—they are particularly good with the Persian mixed herb platter (page 54) or wrapped around a slice of "kuku" (pages 72, 75, and 76). They need to be eaten as soon as they are made, so make sure everything else is ready and then cook the flatbreads at the last minute.

2 ³/₄ cups strong white flour, plus extra, for dusting
³/₄ cup strong whole wheat flour
1 tsp sea salt

3 tbsp light olive oil or sunflower oil, plus a little more for greasing
1¹/₄ cups lukewarm water

Place the white and whole wheat flour in a large mixing bowl with the salt and make a well in the middle. Add the oil and mix the flour with your fingers until it resembles rough breadcrumbs. Add the lukewarm water and mix until you have a soft dough.

Tip out on a lightly floured surface and knead for 8 minutes: use the heel of your palm to repeatedly push down on the dough and fold it in on itself until it is smooth and a little less sticky. Put the dough in a bowl, cover with a damp tea towel, and leave to rest for 10 minutes.

Tip the dough back out onto the lightly floured surface. Rub a little oil onto your hands, then divide the dough into 16 even-sized balls. Meanwhile, place a 9-inch-wide frying pan over a medium heat to warm up.

Take a ball, flatten it into a small round disc with your fingers, and dust each side with a little flour. Use a rolling pin to roll it out until it's the same size as the base of your pan. You might need a bit more flour to dust with, as the dough can get sticky as it thins out.

Cook the lavaash in the hot frying pan for around 30 seconds, until it begins to bubble. Turn over and cook for a further 30 seconds. Turn over again and cook for 15 seconds more on each side, or until the dough is cooked all the way through.

Once cooked, cover the lavaash with a clean tea towel to keep it warm while you make the rest, then serve immediately.

Makes 16 flatbreads

Yogurt with beets and mint
Borani-ye laboo

Somewhere between a dip and a salad, this vibrant, fuchsia-colored mezze dish is a wonderfully cheerful addition to any Persian spread. As the small pieces of cooked beets are folded through the yogurt their purple juices streak through it, leaving behind bright magenta swirls. The longer you leave the flavors to infuse, the deeper the color of the final dish (and the more enchanted your guests will be).

To make a more substantial starter, add some lightly toasted walnuts and feta to top. Serve with flatbread or on the side of a rice dish.

2 cups Greek yogurt
½ garlic clove, crushed
½ tsp sea salt
½ tsp black pepper
½ lb pre-cooked beets, diced into ⅓-inch cubes
1 heaped tsp dried mint, plus extra to garnish

For the toppings (optional):
¼ cup feta, crumbled
¼ cup walnuts, toasted and roughly chopped

In a large mixing bowl, combine the yogurt and garlic, and season with the salt and pepper.

Add the beets and dried mint and stir well.

Taste and adjust the seasoning. Crumble over the feta and the walnuts (if you are using them) then finish with a final sprinkle of dried mint, if you like.

Serves 4–6

Yogurt with cucumber and dill
Mast-e khiar

This refreshing cucumber yogurt is loved all over the Middle East. It is often served alongside kebabs or other grilled meats, which according to traditional Persian medicine have a "hot" effect on the body during digestion. The yogurt, cucumber, and mint combination counteracts this by balancing the meal with the requisite coolness. Serve it with some raw vegetables to dip into it, or try it with Dr. Asaf's juicy lamb kebabs (page 182) or Lime and saffron chicken kebabs (page 164).

(pictured bottom right on page 63)

1 medium cucumber
2 cups Greek yogurt
1/2 garlic clove, crushed
2 tsp dried mint
1 tsp chopped fresh dill
1 tbsp golden raisins
1/2 tsp sea salt
1/4 tsp black pepper

Cut the cucumber in half and scoop out the seeds and watery middle with a teaspoon—discard the seeds. Grate the cucumber and squeeze out the excess juices over a bowl or the sink, using your hands.

Mix the cucumber into the yogurt, along with the garlic, mint, dill, golden raisins, salt, and pepper. Stir well, then serve.

Serves 4–6

Yogurt with pomegranate and mint
Mast-e anar

The sharp, tangy combination of pomegranates with cooling yogurt and mint is one that works beautifully with kebabs or any Persian rice dish.

(pictured top right on page 63)

2 cups Greek yogurt
1 tsp dried mint
1¹/₂ tbsp mint leaves, finely chopped
6 tbsp pomegranate seeds

¹/₂ tsp sea salt
¹/₄ tsp black pepper
Extra-virgin olive oil, for drizzling

Mix the yogurt, dried mint, half of the fresh mint, and 5 tablespoons of pomegranate seeds together with the salt and pepper.

Just before serving, sprinkle the remainder of the pomegranate seeds and the rest of the mint on top and finish with a small drizzle of olive oil.

Serves 4–6

Yogurt with spinach and garlic
Borani-ye esfinaj

Packed with green goodness, the earthy, hearty flavor of this side dish goes particularly well with an Eggplant and mushroom tahcheen (page 142) and other Persian rice dishes.

(pictured top left on page 63)

17 oz spinach
2 cups Greek yogurt
¹/₂ garlic clove, crushed

¹/₂ tsp sea salt
¹/₂ tsp black pepper

Place the spinach in a large saucepan and cook over a high heat for 3–4 minutes until it has wilted. Tip the cooked spinach into a colander, leave it to cool, and then squeeze out as much water as possible.

When the spinach is completely cool, add it to the yogurt, along with the garlic, salt, and pepper. Leave for at least 15 minutes before serving.

Serves 4–6

Burnt eggplant and walnut dip
Kaleh kabob

Eggplants are to northern Iranian food what potatoes are to the Irish table—they seem to find their way into every meal and everyone is the happier for it. This regional speciality from Gilan has some affinity with baba ganoush, but here walnuts are used instead of tahini to add a nutty creaminess to the dish. This is best served after it has had a few hours in the fridge for the flavors to develop, so is a great one to make ahead of time and chill until you are ready to eat it. Golpar (see page 24) is worth buying from Iranian stores or online, if you can, as it accentuates both the meaty flavor of the eggplants and the brightness of the pomegranates.

4 or 5 large eggplants
  (about 3 lbs total)
Sea salt
3/4 cup walnuts
2 garlic cloves, crushed
2 tbsp lemon juice
2 tbsp pomegranate molasses
8 basil leaves, finely chopped

8 mint leaves, finely chopped
1/4 tsp golpar (optional)
Black pepper

To garnish:
2 chopped mint leaves
1 tbsp pomegranate seeds

Pre-heat the oven to 425°F.

Pierce the eggplants a few times with a fork and then place on a baking tray on the top shelf of the oven. Cook for about 1 hour, turning once or twice, until the eggplants are black and burnt on the outside.

Remove the eggplants from the oven and leave to cool slightly before removing their skins and placing them in a sieve with a little salt. Leave for 10 minutes, then give them a squeeze to get the excess water out. Roughly chop and set aside.

Grind the walnuts with a pestle and mortar or a spice grinder until they are very fine and have a smooth, nut-butter-like consistency.

Add the walnuts to the eggplants, along with the garlic, lemon juice, pomegranate molasses, basil, mint, golpar (if you are using it), 1 teaspoon of salt, and 1/2 teaspoon of pepper. Mash the mixture together with a fork until everything is evenly combined but the eggplants are still a little lumpy, for texture. Taste and adjust the seasoning and then leave for at least an hour.

Scatter over the chopped mint and pomegranate seeds just before serving.

Serves 4

Chicken livers with pomegranate molasses

In the summer evenings, one of the most popular activities in Tehran is to wander through the neighborhood of Darband in the north of the city, at the foot of the Alborz Mountains, feasting on barbecued meat from the dozens of street stalls that line the tiny cobbled roads. You select the meat you want to eat—for me, it is often chicken livers—and then watch as the vendor threads it onto his skewer and cooks it on hot coals in front of you.

Back in Britain, this home-cooked version satisfies my cravings, and it is simple to make. Cooking the livers with sweet onions and tangy pomegranate molasses gives you a rich, dark sauce that beautifully balances sweet and sour flavors.

1 lb chicken livers
1 large onion, finely sliced
2 tbsp sunflower oil
3 garlic cloves, crushed
2 tbsp pomegranate molasses

Sea salt and black pepper
1 tbsp chopped parsley,
   to garnish
Flatbread or pita, to serve

Begin by prepping your chicken livers. Wash them under running water. Use a small, sharp knife to remove and discard any white sinew, which can make the dish taste bitter. Chop any large pieces in half so you have even-sized pieces to cook.

Fry the onion in a couple of tablespoons of oil over a low heat until it is soft and translucent. This should take about 10 minutes. Add the garlic and fry for another 2 minutes.

Add the chicken livers and pomegranate molasses to the pan and season well with salt and pepper. Gently fry for 5–8 minutes, until the livers are just cooked through.

Garnish with some chopped parsley and serve immediately, with some flatbread or pita alongside.

Serves 4 as a starter or 2 as a main

Gilaki
pinto beans
Loobia pokhte

These comforting rustic beans are eaten across rural Iran but are particularly popular in the Caspian region, where the local cuisine relies heavily on beans and pulses. Enjoy them as a side, as a main with some bread or rice, or with a fried egg for breakfast—they make a delicious alternative to baked beans. As the cooking times of beans can vary depending on their age, you may need to add a bit more water or cook the beans for a little longer until they are soft and plump.

1 cup dried pinto or rose coco beans (soaked in cold water for 8 hours or overnight)
1 medium onion, quartered
$\frac{1}{2}$ tsp turmeric
1 tsp black pepper
1 tsp sea salt
Juice of 1 lemon
4 tbsp extra-virgin olive oil, plus extra for drizzling
$\frac{1}{2}$ tsp golpar (optional)
1 tbsp tomato purée
1–2 tsp sumac, to garnish

Drain and rinse your soaked beans, then tip them into a large saucepan with a lid. Add the onion, turmeric, and pepper. Pour in enough hot water to cover everything by 2 inches and place over a medium heat.

Bring to the boil, skim off any froth, then reduce the heat and simmer with the lid on for $1\frac{1}{2}$ hours, or until the beans are soft and easily squashable. Halfway through the cooking, add the salt. If the beans start to dry out, add a bit more water.

Take a fork and gently mash the onion against the side of the pan, then stir it back in. Add the lemon juice, olive oil, golpar (if you are using it), and tomato purée and stir well. Cook for another 15 minutes, then taste and adjust the seasoning to taste. Turn up the heat if you want a thicker sauce or add more water if you prefer it a bit thinner.

Drizzle each portion with a little more olive oil and a sprinkle of sumac just before serving.

Serves 4 as a main or 6 as part of a mezze

Corn with sumac
and za'atar spiced butter
Balaal

Traditional Iranian fast food is incredibly healthy and it is not uncommon to see street stalls selling simple steamed or boiled corn, pumpkin, and beets with just a light dusting of spice. Corn is without doubt the most ubiquitous street snack, and as dusk falls in the major cities across Iran, stalls emerge selling little paper cups of corn, which you can douse with sumac, ground red chile, dried thyme, and a gooey mozzarella-style cheese. Roasting the cobs over a gas flame—just like my mum used to do for us at home—gives them bite. The sharp tangy za'atar (a Middle Eastern spice blend of thyme, sumac, and sesame seeds) and deep red sumac add a burst of color and flavor to the butter, which makes the corn taste irresistible.

5 ½ tbsp butter
1 tsp sumac
1 tsp za'atar
¼ tsp sea salt

Black pepper
4 corn cobs, husks and silky
    threads removed

Melt the butter in a small saucepan and add the sumac, za'atar, salt, and a generous grind of pepper. Set aside.

Pre-heat the oven to 275°F and have a baking tray and some foil ready to keep the cobs warm.

Using a pair of metal tongs, cook each cob over a medium-high gas flame (or on the barbecue) until the kernels start to blacken and pop. This should take around 6 minutes per cob.

Wrap the cob in foil and place on the baking tray in the oven to keep warm while you finish cooking the rest. Just before serving, gently reheat the spiced butter and spoon over each corn cob. Serve immediately.

Serves 4

Mixed herb kuku
Kuku-ye sabzi

This Iranian frittata is a sensational deep green color and tastes like spring on a plate, bursting with fresh herby flavor. It is incredibly quick to throw together, will keep for a few days in the fridge, and can be enjoyed hot or cold. Serve as an appetizer or as part of a mezze spread, wrapped up in flatbread with some slices of tomato and a few salty and sour fermented cucumber pickles, or add some crumbled feta and lightly toasted walnuts for a more substantial main.

7 oz spinach
1 medium bunch parsley
1 medium bunch dill
1 medium bunch cilantro
1 medium bunch chives
8 medium eggs
½ tsp turmeric
2 tbsp all-purpose flour

1 tsp sea salt
1 tsp black pepper
1 tsp dried fenugreek leaf
  (see page 24)
2 tsp sunflower oil
3 medium spring onions, trimmed
  and finely chopped
2 garlic cloves, crushed

Wash the spinach, parsley, dill, cilantro, and chives, then dry well on paper towels or in a salad spinner. Try and squeeze as much moisture out as possible; if the greens are wet when they are cooked, they will make the kuku go spongy. Chop finely or blitz in the food processor, in a couple of batches.

Pre-heat the grill to high. Crack the eggs into a large mixing bowl. Add the turmeric, flour, salt, pepper, and fenugreek leaf. Stir in the chopped spinach and herbs.

Heat the oil in a large frying pan. Add the spring onions and garlic and gently fry over a low heat for 2 minutes to soften.

Make sure the garlic and spring onions are evenly distributed around the pan, then pour in the egg mixture. Cook over a low heat for about 5–8 minutes, until the kuku is almost cooked through. Finish off under the hot grill.

Leave to cool slightly, then cut into triangular slices to serve.

Serves 4 as a main or 8 as a starter

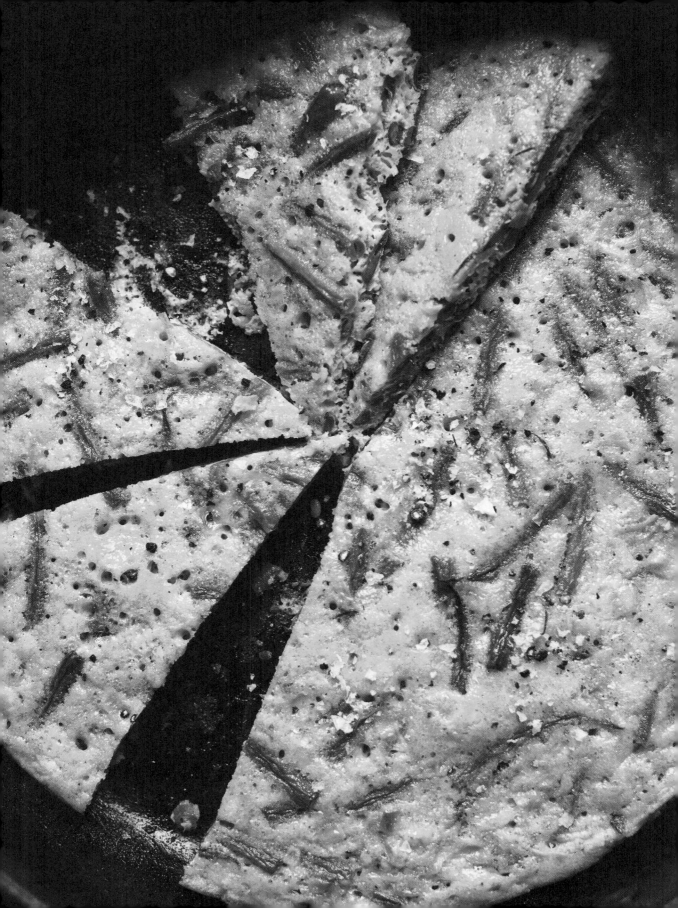

Green bean and caramelized onion kuku

Kuku-ye loobia sabz

This recipe is a great way to use up a glut of green beans. Here they are delicately combined with the mellow sweetness of slow-cooked onions for a tantalizing and colorful kuku. I like to use French green beans, as I find they keep their texture and I prefer a bit of a crunch, but you can substitute any type of green beans or even some podded fava beans, if you have an abundance of them. Enjoy warm or cold, with some bread and a simple green salad.

1 tbsp butter
2 tbsp sunflower oil
2 medium onions, finely chopped
$2/3$ lb (9 oz) green beans, cut into 1-inch lengths
2 garlic cloves, crushed

6 medium eggs
$1/2$ tsp turmeric
1 tsp baking powder
1 tbsp all-purpose flour
$3/4$ tsp sea salt
$1/2$ tsp black pepper

Heat a frying pan with the butter and the oil until the butter begins to foam. Add the onions and gently fry on a low heat for 15–20 minutes, until they are brown and soft.

Place the beans in a pot of boiling water. Cook for 8 minutes or until the beans are tender but still have a bit of a bite. Drain, rinse in cold water to stop them cooking any further, and set aside.

Once your onions are cooked, add the garlic to the frying pan and cook for a further 2 minutes. Remove the onions and garlic from the pan and place in a large bowl to cool. You can use some of the oil that the onions fried in later—so, if you like, squeeze the onions against the side of the bowl and pour the oil back into the pan.

Pre-heat the grill to high. Whisk the eggs, turmeric, baking powder, and flour together in a large mixing bowl, then season with the salt and pepper. Fold in the beans, onions, and garlic.

Put the frying pan on a low heat, adding a bit more oil if you need it. Pour the kuku in and cook with a lid on for about 8–10 minutes, until it is just cooked through. Finish off under the grill so the kuku is set. If you like, scatter the top with flakes of sea salt and a twist of black pepper.

Serves 4 as a main or 6 as part of a mezze

Saffron, potato, and barberry kuku
Kuku-ye sibzameeni

Potato kuku is a popular sandwich filling in Iran. Traditionally the potatoes are grated and then bound together with a little egg and fried like a rosti, but my baked version uses mashed potato and barberries (see page 23) to give the kuku a lighter and creamier texture. You can bake individual kukus in a muffin tin, or make one large kuku to slice at the table. Serve warm or cold with some salad, salty Middle Eastern cucumber pickles, and bread as a satisfying starter or simple, light meal.

Butter, for greasing
A pinch of saffron strands
A pinch of sugar
2 tbsp freshly boiled water
Sea salt and black pepper
2 large potatoes, peeled and cut into 1-inch dice
1 large onion, finely chopped
2 tbsp sunflower oil

1 garlic clove, crushed
5 medium eggs
1 tbsp barberries, washed and soaked for a few minutes in hot water
¼ tsp turmeric
1 tbsp all-purpose flour
1 tsp baking powder
3 tbsp fresh parsley, finely chopped

Pre-heat the oven to 375°F and line a 12-cup muffin tin or an 8-inch square baking pan with lightly greased parchment paper.

Make a saffron liquid by grinding the saffron strands and a pinch of sugar with a pestle and mortar and then adding the boiled water. Leave to steep.

Tip the potatoes into a pan of amply salted water. Bring to a boil, then turn down the heat and simmer until the potatoes are tender, about 12 minutes. Drain well, then roughly mash and set aside to cool.

While the potatoes are cooking, fry the onion in the oil for 10–15 minutes, until it is soft and golden. Add the garlic and fry for 2 minutes more, until it is lightly cooked. Set aside to cool.

Crack the eggs into a large bowl and lightly whisk them. Add the potatoes, onion and garlic, barberries, turmeric, flour, baking powder, parsley, and saffron liquid. Add a teaspoon of salt and ½ teaspoon of pepper and mix well to combine.

Pour your kuku mixture into the prepared tin and bake for around 12–15 minutes, until risen and cooked through.

Serves 4–6

Herby baked falafels with a fennel and watercress salad

Falafels are a street-food staple in Iran, particularly around the Persian Gulf, where the local cuisine borrows heavily from the country's Arab neighbors. Making your own is incredibly simple, especially if you use canned chickpeas.

I've packed this recipe with heaps of fresh herbs and punchy garlic, and the falafels are baked rather than deep-fried, making them a healthy version of the classic Middle Eastern snack. Just make sure you cook the falafels in a very hot oven so they get nice and crispy on the outside and fluffy within. Serve with a crisp fennel and watercress salad, tahini sauce, and perhaps some warm flatbreads and pickles.

1 small bunch parsley
1 small bunch cilantro
4 garlic cloves, crushed
4 spring onions, trimmed
   and roughly chopped
2 x 15-oz cans of chickpeas,
   rinsed and drained
½ tsp cumin seeds
½ tsp cilantro seeds
Zest of ½ unwaxed lemon
2 tbsp lemon juice
1 tsp baking powder
2 tbsp cornflour
Olive oil
1 tsp sea salt
¼ tsp black pepper
2 tbsp sesame seeds

For the tahini sauce:
¼ cup + 1 tbsp tahini
3 tbsp water
2 tbsp lemon juice
½ tsp sea salt

For the fennel and watercress salad:
½ fennel bulb, sliced very finely
   lengthways
3 oz watercress
2 tbsp extra-virgin olive oil
2 tbsp lemon juice
1 tsp sumac
½ tsp sea salt
¼ tsp black pepper

Blitz the herbs, garlic, and spring onion in a food processor until very finely chopped. Add the chickpeas and pulse until evenly combined and fairly smooth. Spoon the mixture into a large bowl.

Dry fry the cumin and cilantro seeds in a small pan over a low heat for a minute or so, then grind with a pestle and mortar or a spice grinder.

Add the cumin, cilantro seeds, lemon zest, lemon juice, baking powder, cornflour, 2 tablespoons of olive oil, the salt, and pepper to the bowl with the chickpea mixture, and use your hands to bring everything together. Cover the bowl with plastic wrap and chill for at least 30 minutes.

Pre-heat the oven to 450°F. Line a large baking tray with parchment paper and lightly grease it with some light olive oil.

Sprinkle the sesame seeds onto a large plate and place 2 tablespoons of olive oil in a small bowl. Roll the falafel mixture into about 16 equal-sized balls. Use your fingers to lightly coat each ball in some oil then sprinkle an even coating of the sesame seeds on each falafel. Place on the baking tray and cook for 30 minutes or so, until the balls are firm and crunchy. Using a spatula, turn half way through, to ensure an even bake.

Meanwhile, make your tahini sauce by whisking all the ingredients together in a small bowl. For the salad, put the fennel and watercress in a bowl, then drizzle over the olive oil, lemon juice, sumac, salt, and pepper, and toss well.

Serve the falafels immediately, with the sauce and salad alongside.

Serves 4

TEHRAN
*Tales of coffee shops
and counter-culture*

The bustling metropolis of Tehran is home to over eight million people
who wrestle the heavy smog and endless traffic jams to eke out a living
in the largest city in the Middle East. It is a place where almost half the
population live below the international poverty line while, on the other
side of town, the city's mega-rich throw extravagant champagne-fueled
pool parties; a place where hard-line clerics gather for Friday morning
prayers to denounce the West, just as Tehrani youth wake up with
hangovers and head to a yoga class. In all these ways and more, Tehran
embodies the complex, contradictory, and sometimes suffocating side
of modern Iran.

Tehran food is equally complex, fusing East and West, traditionalism
and modernity. Upscale restaurants, serving everything from sushi to
chicken waffles, rub shoulders with traditional tea houses serving *dizi*, a
centuries-old lamb, chickpea, and potato stew, cooked in a clay pot over
a fire for several hours until the meat is so tender you can mash it into a
paste with your fork.

After the 1979 Islamic Revolution and the banning of alcohol, all
of Tehran's bars and nightclubs were shut down. Alcohol can still be
bought on the black market, but it comes with exorbitantly high prices
and considerable risk, so today most young Tehranis turn instead to
coffee shops and fast-food joints to meet, eat, and flirt with each other.

Many of the city's hippest cafés also double as small, independent
galleries, showcasing some of the best work from Tehran's burgeoning
arts scene. These include Café 78, a bright and airy space above an art
gallery of the same name, which alongside the usual cappuccinos and

lattes, sells a huge range of *damnoosh* (traditional herbal teas made from plants such as hibiscus and calendula) as well as refreshing liquids known as *aragh*, made from distilled herbs like fennel and willow.

"Serving *damnoosh* and *aragh* are important to us as it is a way of going back to our roots and being proud of what we have as a culture," explains Café 78's owner Mervha Arvin. "All countries have their problems, but when I came back to Iran to open this café after living in the United States for ten years, I wanted to celebrate the good things. I wanted to show young Iranians that it is just as cool to drink traditional Persian drinks like *aragh-e nana* (a sweet, distilled mint extract) as it is to drink Coca-Cola."

All over Tehran, social media is leading the way for foodies to exchange recipes, share pictures of their lunches and post reviews of the hottest new restaurants.

To learn how this new generation of Iranians cook, I spent an afternoon at the home of Faezeh Khorosani, an exuberant young woman who works as a project manager in the city. "The first thing I cooked was rice," Faezeh recalls. "I was nine years old and I had no idea how much to put in the pan. I ended up cooking pretty much all the rice we had in the house and I overcooked it so badly it ended up as lots of little sticky balls!"

These days, Faezeh is a wonderful cook, with a wealth of helpful tips—such as recommending that I mix ground spices into a small cup of hot water before adding them to a stew, so that the flavors are distributed evenly throughout the pan. She also shared with me a delicious recipe

for *Zereshk polo baa morgh* (page 172), a succulent caramelized chicken dish, cooked with sweet and sour barberries and saffron rice.

As Faezeh regaled me with stories of partying with friends and planning her next camping trip, I suggested that her busy life and feisty spirit are not how those outside the country think of Iranian women.

"Iranian women have a strong role in society," she replied. "They are very independent, compared to other women in the Middle East. Every year in recent memory has seen more women going to university than men, and women are getting into higher positions in companies with better salaries. We are not just housewives."

I spent a couple more happy days in Tehran, sharing baked cheesecakes and black Americanos with graphic design students, sipping fresh borage tea with a chart-topping musician, and sampling smoked rice for the first time at the home of a young sculptor. And then there was my visit to Café Ilio—Iran's first artisan chocolatier, where husband and wife team Mehrdad Aghameeri and Sahar Hossein-Najari sell a magnificent selection of truffles, gelato, macaroons, cakes, and jams, handcrafted with a lot of chocolate and even more love.

"We try and keep our products as natural as possible and don't use any artificial flavors," Mehrdad pointed out, insisting that I confirm these claims by sampling the produce myself as he fed me pistachio truffles, sour cherry and chocolate cake, cardamom macaroons, and mulberry and chocolate jam, each morsel tasting more delicious than the last—quite an achievement for a country where people don't traditionally eat any chocolate at all.

Tehran's streets buzz with rebellious energy and underground creativity, which is why I jumped at the chance to visit the home of independent filmmaker Behzad Nalbandi. Iran's film industry is known for its unique cinematography and subtle use of metaphor, and Behzad is a man who embodies this style of creative activity—in his films, and at home in his kitchen.

"Some people say that cooking is an art," he explains, "but for me, it is a way through which I better understand filmmaking. You start with a set of raw ingredients and you have to work out how to put them together. You decide on the theme of your dish, its genre—is it a soup, a stew, a grill? Then you have to work out how to make your ingredients fit your genre and how to make the dish tasty. Sometimes you watch a film and the basic ingredients are all good—the acting, the location, the script, the camerawork—but somehow the film doesn't work, it doesn't move you, it's lacking something. I'd say the film is *bee namak* (without salt). It needs more seasoning."

As Behzad and I cooked together and then ate a dish of *Addas polo*, a soothing, layered rice dish made with lentils and dried fruit (page 148), I reflected that there is certainly nothing *bee namak* about life in Tehran, Iran's most secular and liberal city, which continuously surprises with its juxtaposition of old and new.

SALADS

A BIG BOWL OF crisp salad or a platter of aromatic green herbs and radishes are an essential component of every Persian meal, adding a welcome crunch and freshness to complement the hearty stews and gentle rice dishes.

Traditional Persian salads tend to be very simple—a medley of romaine lettuce, sweet tomatoes, diced cucumber, grated carrots, and perhaps some thin slivers of raw red cabbage, doused with olive oil and lemon juice.

At big family gatherings when I was a child, my cousins and I were often in charge of prepping and dressing the salads and my younger cousin Siamak was particularly adept at getting the level of acidity in a dressing just right. The two of us would spend an inordinate amount of time taste-testing our salads once they were dressed, adding lemon juice drop by drop until the sharpness was just right. It is important to taste dressings and tweak them to your preference, so don't be too rigid about the measurements in this chapter; taste as you go along and add a little more or less of any seasonings and ingredients to suit your taste.

In recent years, the food in Iran's largest cities has increasingly been influenced by Californian cuisine, due to the high proportion of the Iranian diaspora who live there. As a result, many Iranians are getting more creative with their salads, combining seasonal vegetables and fruits with toasted nuts and seeds and making innovative dressings from pomegranate molasses, verjuice, Seville orange juice, and date molasses. I've drawn inspiration from this approach and while some of the recipes that follow are traditional salads that can be served alongside a typical Persian meal, most of them are robust and filling affairs that would make a perfect light lunch or dinner.

Salad Shirazi

The Salad Shirazi is the most common salad in Iran—a cool, crunchy chopped salad that goes perfectly with the soothing stews and luxurious rice dishes of Persian cuisine. It takes its name from the city of Shiraz, the ancient Iranian city of poets and artists, but such is its popularity that it is now eaten throughout the country.

The trick to making a good Salad Shirazi is to cut all your ingredients into similarly small pieces so that when you eat a forkful, you get a taste of everything at once. Aim for equal amounts of cucumber and tomato—it's worth weighing these ingredients out, as sizes of cucumbers and tomatoes do vary. Iranians like this quite sour, so if you want to be really authentic, add a few more squeezes of lemon juice at the end, to taste.

3 small Middle Eastern cucumbers or 1 regular cucumber (around 10 oz)
3 medium-sized tomatoes (around 10 oz), halved and seeds removed
½ red onion
4 radishes, trimmed

For the dressing:
1 tsp dried mint
3 tbsp extra-virgin olive oil
3 tbsp lemon juice
½ tsp sea salt
½ tsp black pepper

If using small cucumbers, halve lengthways. If you have a regular cucumber, peel, halve, and scoop out the seeds inside, using a teaspoon.

Finely dice the cucumber into ⅛-inch cubes. Dice the tomatoes to match. Do the same with the red onion and radishes and tip everything into a large salad bowl.

Whisk the dressing ingredients together, then drizzle over the salad and mix well. Taste and adjust the seasoning, adding more salt or black pepper to your taste. Serve immediately.

Serves 4 as a side

Salad Bandari

In the south of Iran, they make a spicier version of this salad using cilantro and green chiles.

Follow the recipe above but omit the dried mint and instead add a small handful of fresh cilantro and 1–2 green chiles, seeds and pith removed, depending on how spicy you like it and how strong the chiles are.

Cucumber salad
with sekanjibeen dressing

Sekanjibeen is an ancient Persian syrup, concocted from vinegar, sugar, and mint, which can be drizzled over salad leaves, or mixed with ice and water for a refreshing summer drink. My mum used to buy readymade mint sauce and make little bowls of sekanjibeen for us to snack on when the weather turned warm, accompanied by cold, crunchy wedges of lettuce, which we would take it in turns to dip. Here, the classic sekanjibeen flavors brighten up a quick and easy cucumber salad that can be served alongside a barbecue or stew, or eaten as part of a mezze. Keep the cucumber in the fridge until just before assembling the salad so it stays crisp and cool.

For a traditional, lighter snack, simply mix the vinegar, honey, and mint together in a dipping bowl and add some Romaine lettuce leaves on the side, for dipping.

3 tbsp cider vinegar
2 tbsp honey
3 tbsp mint leaves,
    very finely chopped
2 tsp light olive oil
2 regular cucumbers (around 1$\frac{1}{4}$lb)
A handful of pomegranate seeds
$\frac{1}{4}$ tsp sea salt

In a small bowl, whisk together the vinegar, honey, mint, and olive oil.

Cut the cucumbers in half and scoop out the seeds with a teaspoon, then thinly slice on a diagonal into $\frac{1}{4}$-inch slices and place in a serving bowl.

Drizzle over the salad dressing. Sprinkle with a handful of pomegranate seeds and season with the salt. Mix well and serve immediately.

Serves 4–6 as a side

Persian garden salad

This bountiful, healthy salad is my homage to the Persian garden, with its kaleidoscope of colors, textures, and flavors. Iranians love to combine fruit and cheese, and depending on the season you can use either apples or stone fruit here to add a welcome burst of sweetness to the salty feta.

2 handfuls of mixed lettuce leaves
6 cherry tomatoes, halved
1/4 regular cucumber, seeds scooped out, or 1 small Middle Eastern cucumber
1 crisp apple (or a ripe peach or couple of fresh apricots)
8 Iranian or Medjool dates, pitted and roughly chopped
1/2 cup almonds, roughly chopped

3/4 cup feta, crumbled
A handful of basil leaves
4 tbsp (1/4 cup) pomegranate seeds

For the dressing:
1 1/2 tbsp extra-virgin olive oil
1 tbsp lemon juice
1/2 tsp sea salt
1/2 tsp black pepper

Place the lettuce leaves in a large bowl with the tomatoes. Chop the cucumber and fruit into small chunks and add them to the bowl, along with the dates and almonds.

To make the dressing, whisk the olive oil and lemon juice in a small bowl and season with the salt and pepper. Drizzle over the salad and mix well. Taste and adjust the seasoning, adding more salt or black pepper to your taste.

Just before serving, crumble the feta over the salad and top with the basil leaves and pomegranate seeds.

Serves 2 as a main or 4 as a side

New potato salad with a dill yogurt dressing

Soft-boiled potatoes and crunchy cucumber pickles are a winning pair, confirming the theory that often in recipes—as in life—opposites attract. The tangy yogurt and fresh sprigs of dill elevate this from a knee-jerk picnic dish to something altogether more sophisticated. For stand-out punchiness, it is worth getting hold of the Middle Eastern pickled cucumbers, which are salty, sour and crunchy, a world away from soft, sweet gherkins. You can track these down in any Middle Eastern shop or order them online. But if you have no luck, gherkins with little or no sugar will do instead.

1³/₄ lb new potatoes
1 tsp sea salt
¹/₄ lb Middle Eastern pickled cucumbers (or low-sugar gherkins or cornichons)
2 spring onions, trimmed and finely chopped

For the dressing:
4 tbsp Greek yogurt
3 tbsp extra-virgin olive oil
1 garlic clove, crushed
1 tbsp finely chopped dill
¹/₂ tsp sea salt
¹/₂ tsp black pepper

Cut the new potatoes into halves, or so that they are all roughly the same size. Add the salt to a large pot of water and bring it to the boil, then cook the potatoes for 10 minutes or until tender. Drain and set aside to cool.

Dice the pickles into ¹/₃-inch cubes. Place them in a large bowl, along with the cooled potatoes and the spring onion.

To make the dressing, whisk the yogurt, olive oil, garlic, dill, salt, and pepper together and then drizzle it over the potatoes. Mix well, then taste and adjust the seasoning to your preference.

Serves 4

Watermelon, mint, and feta salad

There are few food partnerships so simple yet so successful as that of sweet watermelon with salty feta and fresh mint. My grandparents used to grow watermelons on their farm and many a hot summer's afternoon was spent lounging under a fan in their living room eating the ice-cold fruit they had grown on their land. Ice-cold is still key—there is nothing as limply disappointing as a warm watermelon—so make sure you chill your fruit in the fridge for a good couple of hours before you put this together. It makes all the difference. And please treat the measurements as a guide only; you should add as little or as much mint and feta as you fancy. Some toasted flatbread, to scoop it all up, would go down a treat too.

1 small watermelon (around 1½ lb)
¾ cup feta
A large handful of mint leaves

2 tbsp extra-virgin olive oil
Black pepper

Slice the watermelon flesh into large triangular chunks and arrange them on a serving plate or in a bowl.

Roughly chop the feta into cubes and sprinkle them over the fruit. Add a large handful of mint, drizzle over the olive oil, and season with some freshly ground black pepper. Serve immediately.

Serves 4 as a starter

Carrot and pistachio salad

This refreshing summer salad is a wonderful way to spruce up the humble carrot and was inspired by an afternoon I spent with Leila Rohbani, a yoga teacher from Tehran. I had a delightful time with her, drinking green tea from small stoneware cups and talking about our favorite recipes in the bright, airy rooms of her home, which doubles as her yoga studio—an oasis of calm in the hectic city, overlooking a garden filled with fig and pomegranate trees.

This makes a lovely addition to a mezze spread, or you could serve it with feta and bread for a more substantial meal.

$^3/_4$ lb (about 4 cups grated) carrots, peeled and roughly grated
1 small bunch mint, finely chopped
1 small bunch parsley, finely chopped
2 tbsp lemon juice
3 tbsp extra-virgin olive oil
1 tbsp pomegranate molasses
$^1/_2$ tsp sea salt
$^1/_2$ tsp black pepper
$2^1/_2$ tbsp pistachios, roughly chopped

Combine the carrots, mint, and parsley in a large bowl.

Make the dressing in a small bowl by whisking the lemon juice, olive oil, pomegranate molasses, salt, and pepper together. Pour the dressing over the carrots and stir well. Taste and adjust the seasoning, adding more salt or black pepper to your taste.

Toast the pistachios in a small pan over a medium heat for 1 minute. Sprinkle the nuts over the salad just before serving.

Serves 4

Red cabbage, beet, and date salad

Crunchy raw cabbage is an everyday feature of Iranian salads and in my grandmother's house it was sliced into razor-thin shards and dressed simply with olive oil and lemon juice. Here the cabbage is combined with raw beets and dates for a sweet and healthy take on a winter slaw.

This goes really well with roast chicken or turkey, giving you the option of a lighter addition to a Christmas or Thanksgiving table.

2 medium raw beets, peeled and grated
2 cups red cabbage, finely sliced
1/3 cup Iranian or Medjool dates, pitted and roughly chopped
1 small bunch parsley, finely chopped

For the dressing:
3 tbsp extra-virgin olive oil
3 tbsp lemon juice
1/2 tsp sea salt
1/2 tsp black pepper

Tip the beets into a large bowl, followed by the red cabbage, dates, and parsley.

Whisk the dressing ingredients together in a small bowl. Just before serving, drizzle over the salad and give it all a good toss. Taste and adjust the seasoning, adding more salt or black pepper to your taste.

Serves 4 as a side

Persimmon, goat's cheese, and arugula salad

My family have dozens of persimmon trees on their farm in Iran but as a child I had a real aversion to the fruit, hating the way it tickled my tongue, making it feel dry and fuzzy. It was only as an adult that I learnt that the trick to enjoying persimmons is to hold off until they are so ripe they look like they will burst from their skins. Now, when the fruit is in season, I love to simply chop off the stalks and scoop out the soft, wobbly orange flesh with a teaspoon.

Paired here with walnuts and peppery arugula, persimmons give a sweet, spicy edge to this easy summer salad. If the fruit you buy from the shops isn't quite there yet, let it sit in your fruit bowl until deliciously ripe.

1 tbsp sunflower seeds
$1/4$ cup walnuts, roughly chopped
3 oz arugula
2 ripe persimmons, sliced into
   thin wedges
Scant cup goat's cheese, crumbled

For the dressing:
2 tbsp pomegranate molasses
2 tbsp extra-virgin olive oil
$1/2$ tsp sea salt
Black pepper

Toast the sunflower seeds and the walnuts in a small pan over a medium heat for a few minutes, until they start to look glossy.

For the dressing, whisk together the pomegranate molasses, olive oil, salt, and a generous grind of pepper in a small bowl.

To assemble the salad, start with the arugula, followed by the persimmon, top with the goat's cheese and then add the nuts and seeds. Drizzle over the dressing so it evenly coats the salad and serve immediately.

Serves 2 as a main or 4 as a side

Fragrant mixed herb and flatbread salad
Domaaj

I first sampled this fragrant salad at a small party at the home of Azadeh Sadeghzadeh, a vivacious young fashion designer from Tehran, and it is now one of my staple dishes whenever I am entertaining. I simply place a big bowl of it in the middle of the table and then let my guests help themselves to bowlfuls as we have a few rounds of drinks. It goes down a treat every time.

The salad works best with strips of Persian flatbread (page 60), but if you don't have time to make your own, and can't find any in the shops, then plain tortillas work just as well. The addition of golpar (see page 24), with its citrussy aroma, really lifts this dish, accentuating the sweetness of the pomegranates and adding a wonderful depth of flavor, so try and track some down if you can.

4-5 pieces Persian flatbread
  (or toasted tortillas or pita bread)
$\frac{1}{2}$ cup walnuts, roughly chopped
Scant cup feta, crumbled
1 small bunch mint, roughly chopped
1 small bunch basil, roughly chopped
1 small bunch tarragon, roughly
  chopped
3 tbsp pomegranate seeds,
  to garnish

For the dressing:
2 tbsp balsamic vinegar
3 tbsp extra-virgin olive oil
$\frac{1}{4}$ tsp golpar (optional)
$\frac{1}{2}$ tsp sea salt
$\frac{1}{2}$ tsp black pepper

Using a pair of scissors, cut the flatbread into small jagged pieces and place them in a large bowl.

Toast the walnuts in a small pan over a medium heat for 2 minutes. Add them to the bowl, along with the crumbled cheese and chopped herbs.

To make the dressing, whisk the balsamic vinegar, olive oil, and golpar (if you are using it) with the salt and pepper. Drizzle the dressing over the salad and then get your hands in there, giving the whole thing a good stir to evenly distribute it.

Leave the salad for 10 minutes for the flavors to soak into the bread, then taste and adjust the seasoning. Garnish with a generous sprinkling of pomegranate seeds and finish with a drizzle of extra-virgin olive oil just before serving.

Serves 4 as a starter

Fava bean, sour cherry, and rice salad

This zesty dish is a fusion of two Iranian classics: bagalee polo (layers of rice, fava bean, and dill) and albaloo polo (sour cherry and saffron rice). The best flavors from both dishes are combined here to create a fresh-tasting, wholegrain salad, perfect for a light summer meal.

You can use fresh or frozen fava beans; either way, always slip off their leathery skins. When I was growing up, my mother would plonk a big bag of fava beans in front of me to pop out of their pods while I was watching television. Nowadays, I find the process quite meditative and can recommend settling in with a cup of tea, perhaps with the radio on for company, for a bit of podding therapy.

1 cup brown basmati rice
1 tsp sea salt
1½ cups fava beans, podded
¼ tsp saffron strands
A pinch of sugar
2 tbsp freshly boiled water
Scant cup sliced almonds
½ cup dried sour cherries (or regular dried cherries, or sweetened dried cranberries)
3 tbsp dill, finely chopped
3 tbsp mint leaves, finely chopped
1 spring onion, trimmed and finely chopped
1¼ cups crumbled feta, to garnish (optional)

For the dressing:
4 tbsp extra-virgin olive oil
3 tbsp lemon juice
Zest of ½ unwaxed lemon
½ garlic clove, crushed
1 tsp sea salt
½ tsp black pepper

Wash the rice in several changes of water until it runs clear. Bring a large pot of water to the boil, then cook the rice with a teaspoon of salt until it is soft and tender. Depending on your rice this can take anywhere from 20 to 40 minutes, so follow the instructions on the packet. When it is cooked, drain and rinse in cold water and set aside to cool.

Boil the fava beans for 4 minutes if they are fresh and 6 minutes if they are frozen. To test if they are ready, squeeze one out of its skin and take a bite. It should be soft on the inside but still quite firm outside. Drain the beans and leave to cool, then pop each bean out of its skin. Try and remove the little white stem at the top of each bean too, as it can make the bean taste bitter. Put the beans in a serving bowl.

Make a saffron liquid by grinding the saffron strands with a pinch of sugar using a pestle and mortar. Add the boiled water and leave to steep.

Toast the sliced almonds in a small pan over a low heat for a minute or two, until they start to turn light brown. Remove from the heat and place them in the bowl with the fava beans, along with the sour cherries, chopped herbs, and spring onion.

Take 5 tablespoons of the cooled rice, place it in a small bowl, and mix through the saffron liquid until the rice takes on a golden color from the saffron. Add this saffron rice, along with the remaining brown rice, to the rest of the salad ingredients in the bowl.

Make your dressing by mixing the olive oil, lemon juice, lemon zest, garlic, salt, and pepper. Add the dressing to the bowl and toss well. Taste and adjust the seasoning. If using, crumble the feta over the salad just before serving.

Serves 4

ISFAHAN & SHIRAZ
*Tales of saffron
and rose water*

The cities of Isfahan and Shiraz are the artistic and cultural hubs of Iran, famous throughout the Middle East for their unique Persian-Islamic architecture, intricate patterned tilework, ornate handicrafts, lavishly designed gardens, and masterful poets, such as Hafez and Sa'adi. The region is also home to some of Persian cuisine's most evocative ingredients. Saffron, pomegranates, and roses (for rose water) are all cultivated here. Not only are these store-cupboard essentials for Iranians, but they are also used medicinally, honored in thousand-year-old mythological stories and celebrated in ancient Persian poetry.

The food of central Iran has been shaped by its arid desert climate. In the days before refrigeration, fresh produce quickly perished, and so dried fruits and nuts were often used to enhance main courses. Today, the region's most popular dishes include *albaloo polo*, rice layered with sour cherries and lamb, and *shirin polo*, rice studded with candied carrots, almonds, pistachios, and slivers of orange zest. Sweetness is the dominant taste of the food, so it is no surprise that the country's most sought after desserts originate in these provinces—from soft, chewy pistachio and rose water nougat, known as *gaz*, to *Bastani sonnati*, a thick, saffron custard ice cream, flecked with pistachios (page 213).

My journey through central Iran began in the countryside, visiting the saffron fields and pomegranate orchards of the Esfidani family who had invited me to stay with them. Iran is the largest saffron producer in the world and I arrived just in time for the first days of the harvest in mid-October. Mehri Esfidani, the family matriarch, took me on a tour of her saffron fields early in the morning to show me the crocuses that

were just beginning to open, each proudly displaying their three precious, scarlet stigma. "Saffron flowers bloom for just ten or twelve days each year," Mehri explains. "You have to pick the saffron on the day the flowers open, as by the next day it will be ruined."

Iranians have been using saffron for thousands of years; it is recommended for depression, asthma, reproductive health, blood purification, and even as an aphrodisiac. During our time together, Mehri used it in everything we ate and drank: from infusing a few strands in a pot of tea to pouring a generous amount of saffron liquid into *Gheimeh* (page 178), a lamb, split pea, and dried lime stew, and using it as a marinade for *Jujeh kabob*, tender young poussin barbecued over hot coals (page 164).

With a small cache of saffron wrapped up in my bag as a parting gift, I headed into the city of Isfahan to find out more about this artistic jewel of the Islamic world, and to visit the home of Faranak Evaghi, a design teacher at the local art college. Faranak and I cooked *Ghormeh sabzi*, a rich herb-based lamb stew with red kidney beans and dried limes (page 181). And as we dry fried herbs for the sauce, we talked about the history of the motifs used on the tiles, carpets, ceramics, brassware, and murals that adorn Isfahan—especially the motif of the pomegranate. As an artist, Faranak draws on similar motifs in her own work: "Like many Iranians, pomegranates are my favorite fruit," she explains. "I love the pomegranate tree and the way the blossom goes through so many different shades of pink and red on the way to becoming a pomegranate—the changing colors flicker like flames."

Pomegranates have always been revered in Persian mythology. The hero warrior Isfandiar is said to have eaten the seeds of the pomegranate and become invincible, while ancient Persian Zoroastrian temples would line their gardens with pomegranates trees to symbolize eternal life. "We learn about the beauty of pomegranates from an early age in Iran," Faranak says. "Sometimes people even call their children *anargol*, a term of endearment that means you are as beautiful as the flowers of the pomegranate."

After lunch we walked through the winding, cobbled backstreets of Isfahan's Jolfa district, home to the city's old Armenian and Jewish communities, and filled with boutiques, coffee shops, patisseries, and over a dozen churches. We stopped to sample the pale pink, sweet juice of the first pomegranates of the season and admire the gilded carvings and blue and gold tilework inside the 500-year-old Vank Cathedral. Central Isfahan is an architectural treasure-house, and as we wove our way back to the World Heritage-listed *Naghsh-e Jahan* square, passing beautiful boulevards, picturesque bridges, grand palaces, and elegant mosques, it was easy to feel transported back to the glories of Isfahan's seventeenth-century heyday, when it was the capital of the Safavid-led Persian empire.

My next stop, Shiraz, an ancient and majestic city that dates back at least four thousand years, built a reputation on its literature, poetry, culture, and, at one time, its wine. Shirazi wine used to be the most famous in all of the Middle East and is frequently depicted in Iranian artwork and poetry. Recent archaeological discoveries have found

evidence of wine-making in the region dating back to 4000 B.C., making Shiraz one of the earliest wine producers in the world.

However, since the 1979 Islamic Revolution, the production of alcohol has been banned in Iran, so I knew I wouldn't be visiting any vineyards on this trip. Instead, I happily set off to meet Shaheen Hojabrafkan, a family friend who works as a car salesman. Shaheen was taking me to his favorite hangout, a renowned kebab restaurant called Anaristan, perched high in the hills outside the city.

Anaristan means "pomegranate country" in Farsi, and as we sat on the restaurant's expansive open-air terrace, surrounded by pomegranate orchards, Shaheen talked of the times he'd eaten here with friends: "It was really fun to be here during the last World Cup," he recalled. "We'd watch all the Iran games on big screens while eating our kebabs." This time, we ordered the *kashk-e badinjoon*, a smoky eggplant dip topped with fried onions and *kashk* (fermented whey); as well as the restaurant's speciality, *Mast-e anar* (page 65), a side dish of yogurt with pomegranate and mint that was a delight alongside our lamb fillet kebabs.

A more traditional place to soak up the Shirazi spirit is the garden of Hafez, in the center of the city, where the twelfth-century Persian poet and Sufi mystic is buried. It can be hard to explain the significance of Hafez to non-Iranians. He isn't seen so much as a poet as a divine messenger. No household in Iran is without a copy of his *Divan* (collected works), which many people turn to whenever they have a problem or feel in need of guidance.

The Hafez garden is reportedly one of the best places in town to sample *faloodeh*, the iced rose water sorbet with vermicelli that the town is famous for, so we sat on the steps overlooking Hafez's tomb, eating little bowls of the icy dessert and watching a steady stream of Iranians of all ages and backgrounds walk up to the tomb to pay their respects and offer prayers to this ancient Sufi poet.

With the taste of rose water lingering in my mouth long after we had finished the *faloodeh*, I pondered how deeply embedded the rose is in Persian culture. Roses are indigenous to the country, and the process of distilling the essential oils from the flowers (*attar*) to make perfume and rose water was first developed in Shiraz. In Persian literature, the rose is the symbol of the beloved and is often paired with the nightingale, a bird whose yearning for the rose in Sufi mysticism serves as a metaphor for the soul's yearning for union with God.

Sitting in the sunny Hafez garden, I was overwhelmed by the romanticism of a culture that holds a simple sweet-smelling flower in such high esteem, derives such pleasure from producing intricate artwork, and takes such solace in enchanting poetry.

SOUPS

IRANIAN SOUPS, KNOWN as *aash* in Farsi, are robust and filling, heart-warming concoctions of beans, herbs, vegetables, and perhaps a little meat, cooked in some good-quality broth. Such is the centrality of *aash* in Iranian cooking that the Farsi word for cook is *aashpaz*, which means "soup-maker," and the term for kitchen is *aashpazi khaneh*, which means "soup-house." In many northern parts of the country, a meal always begins with a bowl of soup.

Soups are offered for almost every social and cultural occasion, from a child's birth to funerals. My grandmother bore 11 children and my mother, the eldest, says she always knew when her mum was expecting yet another baby because the neighbors would suddenly turn up with big pots full of pomegranate soup.

Soups have a legendary ability to soothe and comfort, and as such are also often cooked for *nasri*, the Persian custom of taking food to neighbors on the anniversary of a loved one's passing, a tradition that enables people to nourish and connect with each other through the sharing of food.

I adore soup and often make more than I need so I can freeze it in portions, ready for a quick midweek supper. The following recipes are a collection of Iranian classics, along with soups that take inspiration from seasonal produce or highlight a particular Persian spice. Every one of them improves after being left for several hours or overnight to allow the flavors to develop, and so these are great make-ahead dishes.

Legume noodle soup
Aash-e reshte

This nourishing soup is so important to Iranians that every city across the country has cafés and street stalls dedicated to making it, and in the winter months, hungry customers form queues outside the most popular spots. In Isfahan, I tucked into a bowlful in the courtyard of the Abbasi Hotel—reputedly the oldest hotel in the world. Dining there, amid blossoming trees and trickling fountains, it was easy to imagine myself transported back 300 years to when the hotel first opened and weary travelers would have replenished themselves with the same soup.

It is traditional to serve this with a small drizzle of kashk (see page 24)—an umami-flavored fermented whey, which tastes a bit like salted goat's cheese. It is usually available in Middle Eastern stores, but if you can't get hold of any, yogurt is also commonly used as a topping.

3 tbsp sunflower oil
1 medium onion, finely chopped
4 garlic cloves, crushed
1 x 15-oz can of chickpeas, drained and rinsed
1 x 15-oz can of red kidney beans, drained and rinsed
$^3/_4$ cup green lentils, rinsed
$^1/_2$ tbsp turmeric
2 tbsp dried dill
1 tbsp dried mint
1 tbsp dried cilantro
1 tbsp dried fenugreek leaves (see page 24)
2 cups water
4 cups good-quality chicken or vegetable stock
$^1/_4$ lb spaghetti, broken in half

7 oz spinach, roughly chopped
1 small bunch chives, finely chopped
Juice of $^1/_2$ lemon
$1^1/_2$ tbsp soy sauce
3 tbsp extra-virgin olive oil
1 tsp sea salt
1 tsp black pepper

For the toppings:
1 medium onion, finely sliced into half-moons
2 tbsp flour
$^1/_2$ teaspoon sea salt
3 tbsp sunflower oil
about 6 tsp liquid kashk or $^1/_2$ cup Greek yogurt
1 tbsp dried mint

Heat the sunflower oil a large heavy-based pan with a lid. Add the onion and fry over a low heat for 10–15 minutes. When the onion has softened, add the garlic and fry for a further 2 minutes.

Add the chickpeas, beans, lentils, turmeric, dried herbs, and water. Stir and then stick the lid on the pan and leave to simmer over a low heat for 40 minutes. Stir occasionally so the soup doesn't get too dry and stick to the bottom of the pan. If it does, just add another cup of water.

Add the stock to the pan, along with the spaghetti. Bring to the boil, then simmer for about 10 minutes.

Meanwhile, prepare your fried onion topping. Dust the sliced onion with the flour and salt. Heat the oil in a frying pan until it begins to sizzle and then add the onion. Fry over a medium heat for 6–8 minutes until the onion is golden brown and crispy. Set aside on some paper towels to drain and sprinkle over a little more salt.

Next, add the spinach, chives, lemon juice, soy sauce, olive oil, salt, and pepper to your soup. Leave to simmer for a final 10 minutes for the flavors to combine, then taste and adjust the seasoning to your preference.

To serve, pour the soup into bowls and garnish with a drizzle of kashk or a dollop of yogurt. Finish with a sprinkle of the crispy fried onions and a pinch of dried mint.

Serves 4–6

Onion and fenugreek soup
Eshkeneh

According to Iranian legend, this caramelized onion soup is an ancient dish that was fed to soldiers fighting under the Parthian King Arsaces in the third century B.C., to give them power and strength in battle. Some Iranian housewives also claim it is the perfect soup for healing a broken heart, so clearly somewhere along the way the recipe has collected magic powers!

Its unique flavor comes from the dried fenugreek leaf (sometimes labeled "methi"), with its light spiciness and notes of curry leaf. As with all onion soups, the secret to making a tasty batch is to cook the onions long and slow, so take your time with this bit. Serve with some crusty bread.

2 tbsp butter
2 tbsp sunflower oil
4 medium onions (around ³/₄ lb), finely sliced into half-moons
Sea salt and black pepper
2 tbsp cornflour, mixed to a paste with 2 tbsp cold water
5 cups good-quality vegetable or chicken stock
1 tsp turmeric

¹/₂ tsp ground cumin
¹/₂ tsp cayenne pepper
¹/₂ tsp ground cilantro
¹/₂ tsp dried mint
2 tbsp dried fenugreek leaf (see page 24)
1 tbsp fresh lemon juice
4 small eggs
2 tbsp finely chopped parsley, to garnish

Melt the butter with a tablespoon of sunflower oil in a large heavy-based pan. Add the onions and stir well to coat the onions in the oil, then season with a little salt. Gently fry for 30–40 minutes over a low heat, stirring occasionally, until the onions are golden brown and caramelized. If the onions start to dry out, add another glug of oil.

Add the cornflour paste and fry for 2 minutes more.

Add the stock, all the spices, the mint and fenugreek leaf, and the lemon juice and cook for a further 10 minutes.

Taste and adjust the seasoning, adding salt and black pepper to your taste. Then break each egg into a cup and slide into the simmering soup to poach. Cover with a lid for a few minutes, until the egg whites are cooked but the yolks are still a little runny.

Ladle into individual bowls, giving everyone an egg, and sprinkle with finely chopped parsley just before serving.

Serves 4

Pearl barley
and vegetable soup
Soup-e jo

Soup-e jo is the most common starter you will come across in Iranian restaurants up and down the country. It is creamy and grounding, and always served with small wedges of fresh lime alongside, so diners can add their own amount of tartness to the bowl.

Barley grains are a great carrier of robust flavors, and here they are paired with mushrooms and tarragon to deliver an earthy touch. They can soak up a huge amount of water while cooking, so feel free to add a little more water to loosen the soup in the later stages. But don't make it too thin; like most Iranian soups this should have a thick consistency with some bite and texture.

$^1/_3$ cup pearl barley
5 cups good-quality chicken
   or vegetable stock
2 bay leaves
$1^1/_2$ tbsp butter
1 tbsp sunflower oil
1 medium onion, chopped
2 garlic cloves, crushed
1 leek, trimmed and roughly
   chopped
3 carrots, peeled and roughly
   chopped
2 sticks of celery, roughly chopped
$1^1/_2$ cups mushrooms, roughly
   chopped

1 tsp dried thyme
2 cups freshly boiled water
Juice of $1^1/_2$ limes
3 tbsp tarragon, finely chopped
1 tsp sea salt
1 tsp black pepper
$^1/_2$ cup milk

For the toppings:
$^1/_4$ cup natural yogurt
1 tbsp finely chopped parsley
1 or 2 limes, quartered

Place the barley in a saucepan, pour over the stock, and toss in the bay leaves. Cover and cook for $1^1/_4$ hours, stirring occasionally, until the barley is soft.

Melt the butter with the oil in another large saucepan, then add the onion and garlic. Cook for 5 minutes over a medium heat. Add the leek, carrots, celery, mushrooms, and thyme, stir well, then cover with a lid and leave to sweat for 5 minutes.

Scoop the bay leaves out of the pearl barley, then add the barley to the vegetables, along with the water, lime juice, tarragon, salt, and pepper. Cook for 20 minutes more, adding a bit more water if the soup gets too thick. Finally, add the milk and stir through, cooking for a further minute.

Blend the soup in a food processor and then taste and adjust the seasoning. Serve with a dollop of yogurt, some chopped parsley, and a wedge or two of lime.

Serves 4–6

Spicy lentil
and tamarind soup
Soup-e daal addass

Packed with the aromatic spices of southern Iran, this quick and healthy soup brings a cacophony of sour, spicy, and salty flavors—chiles, ginger, tamarind, and cilantro—that make the lentils sing. The consistency is traditionally quite thick, close to that of an Indian dahl, but you can add more or less water, as you prefer. And if you like it very thick, you could always serve it with rice.

Lentils seem to have a mixed reputation, which I suspect is down to not cooking them the right way. All legumes need generous amounts of salt and oil or fat to give them flavor, so don't scrimp on those two things and they will always taste delicious.

1 cup split red lentils, rinsed
4 cups hot water
2 medium onions, finely chopped
1–2 tbsp sunflower oil
2-inch piece (about ⅓ oz) ginger,
   peeled and very finely chopped
4 garlic cloves, crushed
3 oz tamarind pulp (see page 28)
3 tbsp freshly boiled water
½ tsp cilantro seeds

½ tsp cumin seeds
¼ tsp ground cinnamon
¼ tsp cayenne pepper
1 tsp turmeric
4 tbsp tomato purée
2 tbsp extra-virgin olive oil,
   plus extra to drizzle
1½ tsp sea salt
1–2 tbsp finely chopped cilantro,
   to garnish

Put the lentils in a medium-sized saucepan, cover with the hot water, and bring to the boil. Simmer over a medium heat for 20 minutes.

Meanwhile, fry the onions in the oil for about 10 minutes, until soft. Add the ginger and garlic and fry for another 5 minutes.

Place the tamarind in a bowl, pour on the boiling water, and leave to soak for 5 minutes.

Toast the cilantro and cumin seeds in a small pan over a low heat for a minute and then grind into a fine powder with a pestle and mortar or a spice grinder. Add these spices to the lentils, along with the cinnamon, cayenne pepper, turmeric, tomato purée, olive oil, and salt.

Strain the tamarind and its soaking liquid through a sieve, giving the seeds a good rub to get all the pulp off them before discarding. Add the liquid pulp to the soup and stir well, then simmer for 10 minutes to bring all the flavors together.

Take the soup off the heat and blend in a food processor. Serve with a drizzle of olive oil and a sprinkling of chopped cilantro.

Serves 4

Hot yogurt and chickpea soup

Aash-e mast

I discovered this heartwarming soup on my travels around Tabriz in the north-east of Iran, where the cuisine makes judicious use of local dairy products—including (a new discovery for me) yogurt in hot soups. The result is a rich and creamy soup dotted with plump chickpeas that are so soft they practically melt in your mouth.

For this recipe, good-quality stock is essential, as is being careful that the yogurt doesn't split during the final stages. I would recommend the texture of pudding rice over white rice, and advise against skipping the butter or using low-fat yogurt, as the soup needs these elements to bring it together. It can be served immediately or can happily sit for a few hours or overnight to allow the flavors to develop. Serve with bread.

2 tbsp butter
2 tbsp sunflower oil
2 medium onions, finely chopped
3 garlic cloves, crushed
1 x 15-oz can of chickpeas, drained and rinsed
5 cups good-quality chicken or vegetable stock
$^1/_3$ cup pudding rice (or white rice)
2 cups Greek yogurt

$^1/_4$ cup finely chopped chives
$^1/_4$ cup finely chopped dill, plus extra for garnishing
$^1/_4$ cup + 2 tbsp finely chopped parsley
1 tbsp dried mint
1 tbsp cornflour, mixed into a paste with 2 tbsp cold water
1 tsp sea salt
$^1/_2$ tsp black pepper

Melt the butter with the sunflower oil in a large heavy-based pan. Add the onions and fry over a low heat for around 15–20 minutes, until soft and golden. Don't rush this bit, as the caramelized onions create the base of the soup's flavor.

Add the garlic and fry for a few minutes before adding the chickpeas, stock and rice. Cook for 10 minutes more.

Spoon the yogurt into a large bowl, add a couple of ladles of hot soup, and stir to warm through. Take the pan off the heat and slowly add the yogurt mixture, one ladle at a time, so that it doesn't split. Add the fresh and dried herbs, cornflour paste, salt, and pepper.

Place the soup back on the stovetop and simmer over a low heat for 15 minutes, stirring occasionally. Taste for seasoning and serve with a little extra dill sprinkled on top.

Serves 4

Butternut squash and dried lime soup
Soup-e kadoo halva-ee

Pumpkins and squash are very popular in Iran. Their dense orange flesh is so sweet and flavorful that often they are simply steamed in large chunks with their rind still on and served with a sprinkling of salt. Squash is my favorite vegetable, and one that reminds me to enjoy autumn. There is a moment in the first few days of the season when I suddenly relinquish my resistance to the end of summer and transition, quietly, to a celebration of the new harvest, pulling out my trusty woolen sweaters and throwing myself into making a big batch of this soup.

The slight bitterness and citrus aroma of the dried limes perfectly complements the natural sweetness of the squash, adding an elegant flavor. Feel free to use any kind of winter squash or pumpkin here. Just remember that the sweetest ones have a thick rind (if you can push your fingernail into it, the squash is probably immature and lacking in flavor) so make sure you have a large, very sharp knife for chopping.

2 tbsp sunflower oil
2 medium onions, finely chopped
$^1/_4$ tsp cilantro seeds
$^1/_4$ tsp cumin seeds
1 medium (about 2 lb) butternut squash or pumpkin, peeled, deseeded and cut into $^3/_4$-inch chunks
$^1/_4$ tsp ground cinnamon
2 dried limes (see page 23)
2 cups good-quality vegetable stock
$^3/_4$ cup water

Scant tbsp butter
1 tbsp extra-virgin olive oil
1 tbsp pomegranate molasses
Sea salt and black pepper

For the toppings:
$^1/_4$ cup natural yogurt (optional)
A handful of pomegranate seeds (optional)
$^1/_3$ cup pumpkin seeds
Extra-virgin olive oil

Heat the sunflower oil in a large heavy-based pan with a lid. Add the onions and fry for 5–10 minutes until they are soft.

Toast the cilantro and cumin seeds in a small pan over a low heat for a minute, then grind them with a pestle and mortar or a spice grinder. (Set aside the small pan.)

Add the squash or pumpkin to the pan with the onions, followed by the ground spices, and stir well. Stick the lid on and leave to sweat for 5 minutes over a low heat.

Pierce the dried limes with a fork a few times and add to the pan. Pour in the stock and water, cover, and cook for around 15–20 minutes more, or until the root veg is soft.

Meanwhile, prepare the seed topping by toasting the pumpkin seeds in the small pan for a few minutes until the seeds begin to crisp up. Transfer to a bowl to cool.

When the root veg is cooked, squeeze the dried limes against the side of the pan with a wooden spoon until they burst and all their juices flow out. Remove the limes (leaving them in will make the soup taste bitter) and blend in the food processor.

Add the butter, olive oil, and pomegranate molasses and season to taste with salt and pepper.

If you like, spoon a dollop of yogurt into each bowl of soup and sprinkle over some pomegranate seeds. Finish with the pumpkin seeds and a drizzle of olive oil.

Serves 4

Pomegranate soup
Aash-e anar

Bursting with classic Iranian flavors, this hearty, sweet and sour soup combines the earthy sweetness of beets with the sharpness of pomegranate molasses. Thickened with beans and rice, the final dish resembles more of a stew than a soup and as such is a perfect one-pot meal, served with some warm toasted bread. Fresh herbs and a garlicky topping add the obligatory Persian freshness to the meal and any leftover yogurt makes a great dip for crudités or crackers.

Scant cup mung beans
3 tbsp sunflower or light olive oil
2 medium onions, finely chopped
4 garlic cloves, finely chopped
1 tsp cumin seeds
1 tsp turmeric
4 cups water
1/3 cup pudding rice
1 medium beet (about 5 oz), peeled and finely grated
4 tbsp pomegranate molasses
3 cups good-quality chicken or vegetable stock
1 tsp sea salt
1/2 tsp black pepper

1 small bunch parsley, finely chopped
1 small bunch mint, finely chopped
1 medium bunch cilantro, finely chopped
3 tbsp extra-virgin olive oil

For the toppings:
1 garlic clove, crushed
1/2 cup Greek yogurt
3 tbsp cilantro, chopped
1/2 cup walnuts, roughly chopped
3 tbsp pomegranate seeds (optional)

Wash the mung beans and then leave to soak in a large bowl of water for 15 minutes before draining.

Heat the oil in a large heavy-based pan with a lid. Add the onion and fry over a low heat for 10 minutes (with the lid off).

When the onion has softened, add the garlic and fry for a further 2 minutes.

Toast the cumin seeds in a small pan over a low heat for 1 minute. Grind the toasted seeds with a pestle and mortar or a spice grinder, and add to the onion pan along with the turmeric, soaked mung beans, and water. Cover, then simmer for 35 minutes.

Add the rice, beets, pomegranate molasses, stock, salt, and pepper and cook for 20 minutes.

Add the herbs and olive oil and cook for a final 10 minutes. You may need to add a touch more water if the soup is looking a bit thick. Taste and adjust the seasoning to your preference.

When the soup is ready, prepare your toppings. In a small bowl, mix the garlic, yogurt, and cilantro. Lightly toast the walnuts in the small pan over a medium heat for 1 minute.

Serve the soup with a generous dollop of the herby yogurt and finish with the toasted walnuts and the pomegranate seeds, if you are using them.

Serves 4–6

Pistachio soup
Soup-e pisteh

Pistachios are Iran's culinary treasure—no feast or celebration takes place without a big bowl of them on the table, and there is no surer way to a Persian's heart than a gift of top-quality pistachios. This is why you find such large boxes of them in patisseries across Iran, fashioned into heart-shaped arrangements and elaborately wrapped with bright fuchsia bows. What other country in the world would do that for a box of nuts? Here, they are used as the base for this incredibly rich and indulgent soup, which is perfect for special occasions or a festive spread.

1³/₄ cups shelled, unsalted pistachios
2 tbsp butter
1 medium onion, finely chopped
2 garlic cloves, crushed
1 medium leek, trimmed
    and finely chopped
¹/₂ tsp cumin seeds
1 tbsp cornflour, mixed into a paste
    with 2 tbsp cold water
4 cups good-quality chicken stock

¹/₂ tsp sea salt
¹/₂ tsp black pepper
Juice of 1 orange
1¹/₂ tbsp fresh lime juice

For the toppings:
¹/₄ cup Greek yogurt
1 tbsp pistachios, roughly chopped
    and toasted
Sumac

Blanch the pistachios in a pan of boiling water for 2 minutes. Drain and then rub the nuts with your fingers, discarding the purple skins. Rinse in a bowl of hot water to remove any remaining bits of skin.

Melt the butter in a large saucepan and add the onion, garlic, and leek. Fry for 10 minutes until soft.

Toast the cumin seeds in a small pan for a few minutes and then grind with a pestle and mortar or a spice grinder. Add to the pan along with the cornflour paste, stock, salt, and pepper. Leave to simmer for 15 minutes.

Pour the soup and the pistachios into a food processor and blend for at least 3 minutes, until you have a smooth consistency.

Return the soup to the pan and add the orange and lime juice. Heat through, then taste and adjust the seasoning to your preference.

Serve with a swirl of yogurt, a few slivers of toasted pistachios, and a pinch of sumac.

Serves 4

TABRIZ
Tales of milk and honey

For centuries, the city of Tabriz, set in the high mountains of north-west Iran, has been a place of connection, bridging the Caucasus, the Middle East and north-eastern Europe through trade and commerce. It was one of the capitals of ancient Persia and an important stopping point on the old Silk Road, famed for its bustling bazaars selling aromatic spices from India and China, intricate woven carpets, semi-precious stones, and, delicate silks. Modern Tabriz still has a famous bazaar—now a UNESCO World Heritage site—but the rest of the town is less evocative, filled with car factories and petrochemical refineries.

The land surrounding Tabriz is remarkably fertile, with some scholars even suggesting it might have been the location of the Garden of Eden. Certainly it is a land flowing with milk and honey, and the local produce is amongst Iran's best: golden apricots that taste like honey and feel like warm sunshine on your skin; peaches so succulent you barely notice the trickle of sweet juices that run down your chin as you eat them; and small black figs, firm and velvety to the touch, that erupt with jammy stickiness when you tear them open.

Dairy produce is a regional delicacy enjoyed with every meal—from ivory buffalo-milk butter spread on your breakfast bread to thick fermented yogurt drinks for washing down your lunch, and creamy rose-water-infused rice puddings for rounding off your evening meal. Rest assured there is no concern about anyone from these parts not getting their daily calcium requirement.

Another specialty is the famously dark, toffee-tasting local honey and the slabs of amber honeycomb, which locals insist give you the strength

to get through the harsh Tabrizi winters. On a cold February morning, I waded through thick snow to visit Khoradar Kiana, a beekeeper in the village of Kandavan, just outside Tabriz. Kandavan is a thirteenth-century village whose inhabitants live in homes built into caves formed of volcanic rock. "My family have been living here in the mountains for eight hundred years. We survive by eating food like this local honey, which is rich and sustaining," Khoradar explained, tempting me with samples from three metal vats filled with different types of honey—each one a different shade of caramel, the chewy honeycomb getting quickly stuck between my teeth. Convinced, I bought a disc of honeycomb the size of an LP as a gift to take home to my family. On my way out of the shop, Khoradar shared a tip: "We use the honey in jams too. Plum jam and rose-petal jam made with honey are delicious."

It is clear that this is the guiding principle of Tabrizi cuisine. Food which is *moghavee*—sustaining and energy-giving—is necessary for a city that endures tough winters with daytime temperatures hovering close to freezing. So I sample *Aash-e anar* (page 124), a hearty rice, pomegranate, and lentil soup flavored with massive handfuls of dill and mint; *borsht*, a stew of beets, potato, and cabbage, cooked slowly in a rich beef broth; and all kinds of the seasonal stuffed vegetables known as *Dolmeh* (page 146).

At the home of university lecturer and nutritionist Parveen Pourabdollahi, I spent a morning learning how to make Tabriz's prized *dolmeh*. Stuffing eggplants and peppers with a lamb and rice mixture infused with cumin, chile, and rose petals, we reflected on the different eating habits of our respective countries. "Eating together is a really important social custom

in Iran," Parveen notes, "but *ahdab-e ghazah khordan* (the customary way of eating) is being lost. When I was a child, no matter how hungry we were, we would always wait for all the members of the family to be together before eating. Nowadays, the husband and wife might eat something together and then the kids might grab something on their own. The concept of gathering to eat a family meal is gone."

As a nutritionist, Parveen laments this change, "You see, eating isn't just about filling your stomach," she points out. "It is an opportunity to sit with one another, to talk about your day, to share your problems, your thoughts, your feelings. This is one of the most important reasons why we cook—so we can share our food and our time with our loved ones."

At the house of Batool Mohamdipour—or Maman Betty, as she insisted I call her—the custom of sharing food is still strong. Maman Betty is a warm-hearted grandmother, one of those instinctive cooks with a magic touch, who just knows how to make food taste good. She moved slowly but purposefully around her kitchen, as she shared her tips on how to make *Gheysavah*, a sweet date omelette spiced with ginger and cinnamon (page 36), in broken Farsi.

The East Azerbaijan province of Iran is home to over ten million Azeris, who speak their own language (a dialect of Turkish). "My family are from Tabriz but my husband was originally from what is now Azerbaijan," Maman Betty explains. "He knew how to read and write Azeri, Turkish, Russian, and Latin—he learned them at school—but not Farsi, so we only spoke Azeri at home. That is why my Farsi isn't very good." Happily, the language of the kitchen has a fluency across cultures,

and soon we were sizzling soft dates in the local butter as Maman Betty prepared her next dish: a huge pot of Hot yogurt and chickpea soup (page 121) for lunch.

Later that day, her granddaughter Yasaman took me out to explore the city's street food. Starting in El Goli park, a beautifully designed Persian garden set around a small lake, we tucked into steamed beets, cooked simply with some sugar and salted water along with *sambuse*, flatbread filled with steaming hot mashed potato, topped with a big slab of fresh golden butter, a crushed boiled egg, and a sprinkling of grassy dried mint.

"This is classic workers' food," Yasaman pointed out. "The people in the markets eat it most days when the weather is cold and they want something filling." And I nodded, feeling the warmth radiating from my belly as my feet crunched through the snow.

Later, we headed to a *sofreh-khaneh*, a traditional shisha café, where Yasaman introduced me to her friends, who drink tea, eat baklava, and smoke shishas flavored with orange, mint, and apple. They are a raucous bunch and as I lazed on the cushions, they regaled me with stories and gossip, and pouted for Instagram photos. "Girls in Iran aren't usually allowed to smoke shisha on their own," Yasaman explained. "You normally need to have a man with you. But this place lets us hang out on our own without any hassle, so we come here a few times a week."

We shared the shisha pipe between us, sipping small cups of black tea. Tearing through plate after plate of crisp walnut and pistachio baklavas, cut into dainty rectangles or diamonds and dripping with sugar syrup, I relished sharing an ancient ritual with these very modern girls.

MAINS

IRANIAN MAIN COURSES broadly fall into three main categories: layered rice dishes, deeply aromatic stews known as *khoresht*, and grills.

Elegant grains of light, dry, fluffy rice are a hallmark of Persian cuisine, where cooking rice is elevated to an art form. Rice takes center stage at meals, served either plainly—steamed with a buttery saffron crust—or layered with vegetables, meat, herbs, and spices for a more elaborate *polo*.

The magic of *khoresht* lies in their tantalizing and uniquely Persian combinations of meat, fruit, vegetables, pulses, and nuts, adorned with lots of fresh and dried herbs. There is something deeply comforting and nourishing about these one-pot dishes. Ingredients that might overwhelm if eaten separately relax as they get to know each other, quietly bubbling away on a stove for a few hours until their flavors blend harmoniously together.

Traditionally, only small amounts of meat are added to flavor *khoresht* and so many of them work just as well without it. All *khoresht* taste better the day after, which means they are easy to make in advance. They are traditionally served with plain rice and plenty of natural yogurt on the side, but there is nothing to stop you substituting another grain of your choice.

Iranians love a good barbecue, and grilled meat and fish are often what people turn to when they eat out in Iran. I pay homage to some of my favorite regional grilled dishes in this chapter, with recipes that are just as tasty made indoors in an oven or under a grill as they are cooked over hot coals.

Persian rice
Chelow

This is the master recipe for one of Iran's classic dishes: perfectly steamed, elongated grains of rice with a buttery saffron crust. The rice is first soaked, then parboiled, then steamed very slowly. (For many Iranians, the best part of this dish is the crisp crust that forms at the bottom of the pan during cooking—the "tahdig".) To finish, the contents of the pan are carefully turned out, producing an elegant golden rice cake.

There is no specific water-to-rice ratio here, so you can cook any amount of rice by following this method. Just be sure to use a heavy-based, nonstick pan with a snug-fitting lid (see page 27 for my specific recommendation) and have a clean tea towel or some paper towels to hand, for lining the lid.

To make this recipe dairy-free, simply replace the butter with a tablespoon more of sunflower oil.

1¾ cups white basmati rice
Sea salt
A pinch of saffron strands
A pinch of sugar

2 tbsp freshly boiled water
1 tbsp butter
1½ tbsp sunflower oil

Rinse the rice in several changes of cold water until the water runs clear, then leave to soak in a large bowl of water for 15 minutes. Drain and set aside.

Bring a large pot of water to the boil and add 2 tablespoons of salt. (Don't worry about the large amount of salt here, the rice has a very short time to absorb the water and the final result won't be too salty.) Add the rice and cook for 4–5 minutes over a medium heat. Taste to test; the rice should be soft on the outside but still hard and firm in the middle. Drain, then rinse with tepid water to stop it cooking any further and set aside.

Make a saffron liquid by using a pestle and mortar to grind the saffron strands with a pinch of sugar (picture 1, overleaf) and then adding the boiled water. Leave to steep.

To make a plain tahdig for this amount of rice, you need an 8-inch nonstick saucepan with a snug-fitting lid. Melt half of the butter with the sunflower oil over a medium heat. Add 1 tablespoon of the saffron liquid and season with a pinch of salt. When the oil is hot, sprinkle a thin layer of rice over the bottom and firmly press it down to line the base of the pan. Using a large spoon, gently layer the rest of the rice on top, building it up into a pyramid shape so that it does not stick to the sides (picture 2, overleaf).

Using the handle of a wooden spoon, make four holes in the rice, almost but not quite down to the bottom of the pan. Dot the rest of the butter into these holes. Spoon over the remaining saffron liquid (picture 3, overleaf) and then place a clean tea towel or four layers of paper towels on top of the saucepan and put the lid on tightly (picture 4, overleaf). Tuck in the edges of the tea towel, or trim the edges of the paper towels to fit, so they won't catch fire.

Cook the rice over a medium heat for 5 minutes and then turn the heat down to very low and cook for 15 minutes.

When the rice has cooked for its allotted time, take it off the heat and leave it to stand for a few minutes.

(continued on page 140)

(continued from page 136)

Fill the sink with an inch or two of cold water and place the saucepan, with the lid still tightly on it, in the water. The rush of steam this produces will loosen the crust at the bottom of the pan. Take the saucepan out of the water and place a large plate over the top. Quickly and deftly turn the rice out onto the plate (picture 5, previous page).

If all goes to plan, you should have a beautiful cake-shaped mound of rice with a crispy top. If not, don't worry, practice makes perfect. If your crust comes out soft, turn the heat up a little at the start of the cooking next time. If the crust is slightly burnt, reduce the heat at the initial stage of cooking.

You can also use additional ingredients to add texture and extra crispness to the crust. Below are some of my favorites.

Flatbread tahdig

Using a disc of unleavened flatbread will give you the crunchiest tahdig; this is the version I always use for a special occasion. Start by parboiling the rice and making the saffron liquid. Cut some Persian flatbread (page 60) or a tortilla to the size of the base of your saucepan. After you have heated the butter, oil, and saffron in your pan, season with a little salt and then place the flat disc of bread on the bottom of the pot. Gently layer the parboiled rice onto the bread using a large spoon, then finish the rice as usual.

Potato tahdig

Crispy fried potatoes make everything taste better, and Persian rice is no exception. Start by parboiling the rice and making the saffron liquid. After you have heated the butter, oil, and saffron in your saucepan, season with a little salt and then place thin slices of peeled potato at the bottom of your pan. Gently layer the parboiled rice on top, then finish the rice as usual.

Yogurt tahdig

Using yogurt stops the tahdig from sticking to the bottom of the pan and produces a slightly moister crust. Start by parboiling the rice and making the saffron liquid. Take 5 tablespoons of parboiled rice and mix it with 3 tablespoons of natural yogurt. After you have heated the butter, oil, and saffron, season with a little salt and spread the yogurt and rice mixture across the base of your pan. Layer the remaining rice into the pan, then finish the rice as usual.

Plain tahdig

Flatbread tahdig

Potato tahdig

Yogurt tahdig

Eggplant and mushroom tahcheen

This beautiful, saffron-infused savory rice cake is a regional speciality from Shiraz in central Iran. Traditionally it is made with poached chicken, but this vegetarian alternative swaps in rich and earthy Portobello mushrooms and meaty eggplants. Tahcheen is a great dish to make if you are entertaining, as you can prepare everything in advance and then simply put it in the oven a few hours before your guests arrive. It makes a substantial meal with a Salad Shirazi (page 88) and Yogurt with spinach and garlic (page 65) but if you fancy some meat then roast chicken would be a delicious addition too.

2 cups white basmati rice

1¼ tsp saffron strands

A pinch of sugar

3 tbsp freshly boiled water

3 medium eggplants
   (around 1¼ lb), cut lengthways
   into 1-inch slices

Sea salt and black pepper

Sunflower oil

3 tbsp butter

1 medium onion, finely chopped

3 garlic cloves, crushed

4 Portobello mushrooms,
   sliced into large chunks

½ tsp turmeric

½ tsp allspice

¼ tsp cinnamon

¼ tsp cayenne pepper

½ tsp cumin seeds

2 egg yolks

¾ cup Greek yogurt

For the topping:

1 tbsp butter

2 tbsp barberries

¼ cup + 1 tbsp pistachios, roughly
   chopped

1 tbsp sugar

Pre-heat your grill to medium-high. Rinse and parboil the rice and prepare the saffron liquid, following the method on page 136.

Drizzle the eggplant slices with some sunflower oil and season generously with salt. Grill for 10–15 minutes, turning occasionally, until the eggplants are cooked through.

Meanwhile, make the rest of your filling. Heat 2 tablespoons of sunflower oil with 1 tablespoon of the butter in a large saucepan and fry the onion for about 10 minutes, until soft. Add the garlic and fry for a further 2 minutes.

Add the mushrooms to the pan along with the turmeric, allspice, cinnamon, cayenne pepper, 1 teaspoon of salt, and ¼ teaspoon of pepper. Lightly toast the cumin seeds in a small pan for a minute and then crush them with a pestle and mortar or a spice grinder, and add them too. Cook until the mushrooms are soft and then take off the heat.

Pre-heat the oven to 375°F. In a large bowl, beat the egg yolks with the yogurt, saffron liquid, 1½ teaspoons of salt, and 1 teaspoon of pepper. Fold the rice in until it is evenly coated with the yogurt and saffron.

Rub 1 tablespoon butter over the base and sides of a 10-cup ovenproof glass dish. Spoon half of the rice into the dish and press it down evenly. Add a layer of eggplants and mushrooms and finish with a final layer of rice. Dot with the remaining butter, cover the dish tightly with foil, and bake for 1½–2 hours or until the base of the tahcheen is crisp and golden brown.

When the tahcheen is ready, remove from the oven and leave to cool slightly while you make your topping. Melt the butter in a small frying pan and fry the barberries, pistachios, and sugar for 2 minutes until the sugar has melted and the dried fruit has plumped up.

To serve, run a butter knife around the sides of the tahcheen to separate it from the dish. Place a large board over the top and quickly invert the whole thing. Garnish with a sprinkling of the barberry and pistachio topping.

Serves 6

Smoky eggplants with egg and tomato
Mirzeh ghasemi

This smoky eggplant dish is a regional speciality from the Gilan province and brings back happy memories for me. My Auntie Tahereh still makes the best version I've ever tasted, packed with garlic and dripping with olive oil. There's always a ripple of excitement in the house when we hear she is cooking it, and the smell of sizzling garlic makes our mouths water in anticipation.

These instructions are for cooking inside, but you can of course grill the eggplants on the barbecue—traditionally they are cooked over coals until burnt, giving them an intensely smoky flavor. Serve them as part of a mezze, with rice or warm bread as a light meal, or alongside a hearty dish such as Garlicky beans with dill and egg (page 151).

4 or 5 large eggplants
   (at least 3 lb before cooking)
Sea salt and black pepper
Sunflower oil
4 large garlic cloves, crushed
$\frac{1}{2}$ tsp turmeric

1 medium tomato
1 tsp tomato purée
1$\frac{1}{2}$ tbsp extra-virgin olive oil,
   plus extra for drizzling
2 medium eggs
1 tbsp chopped parsley, to garnish

Pre-heat the oven to 425°F.

Pierce the eggplants a few times with a fork and then place on a baking tray. Cook on the top shelf of the oven for about 1 hour, turning once or twice, until the eggplants are totally black and burnt on the outside and have collapsed in on themselves.

Remove the eggplants from the oven and leave to cool slightly before removing their skins. Sprinkle with salt, place in a sieve, and leave for 10 minutes, then squeeze out the excess water. Roughly chop and set aside.

Heat 2 tablespoons of sunflower oil in a frying pan over a medium heat. Add the garlic and fry for a minute. Add the eggplant, turmeric, $\frac{3}{4}$ teaspoon of salt, and $\frac{1}{2}$ teaspoon of pepper, and then turn the heat up and fry the eggplant for 10 minutes. Stir regularly so the eggplant doesn't stick to the bottom of the pan.

Use a sharp knife to score a small cross into the base and top of the tomato. Place it in a bowl of just boiled water for about a minute. Drain well—the skin should now rub off easily. Cut the tomato in half, remove and discard the seeds, and chop into medium-sized chunks. Add the tomato to the frying pan, along with the tomato purée and olive oil. Cook for a further 5 minutes until most of the water from the tomatoes has evaporated.

Using a wooden spoon, burrow two egg-sized holes in the eggplant mixture and crack the eggs into them. Leave the eggs to cook for a minute and then run your spoon through the yolks so they break into the eggplant. Don't mix too much as you want chunks of egg in the finished dish.

When the eggs are cooked, the dish is ready to serve. Adjust the seasoning with salt and pepper to your taste, drizzle over some olive oil, and garnish with fresh parsley.

Serves 4 as part of a mezze or 2 as a main

Stuffed eggplants
Dolmeh

Stuffing vegetables is a regional hobby in north-western Iran and each family has their own time-honoured techniques for stuffing a variety of squashes, peppers, tomatoes, potatoes, and vine leaves. Parveen Pourabdollahi, an effervescent university lecturer in nutrition from Tabriz, taught me hers while rushing around her kitchen at breakneck speed, lamenting the demise of traditional cooking skills amongst young Iranians and the encroachment of fast-food joints on every corner. Well, I'll be honest, there is nothing speedy about this recipe, but sometimes the best dishes come to those who wait. Serve with salad and crusty bread.

2 large eggplants (about $1\frac{1}{2}$ lb)
Extra-virgin olive oil
Sea salt and black pepper
$\frac{1}{4}$ cup puy lentils, rinsed
Sunflower oil
2 medium onions,
  very finely chopped
5 garlic cloves, crushed
$\frac{1}{2}$ cup pudding rice
1 cup good-quality vegetable stock
$\frac{1}{4}$ tsp turmeric
$\frac{1}{4}$ tsp ground cinnamon
A pinch of cayenne pepper
$\frac{1}{2}$ cup hot water

2 tbsp tomato purée
$\frac{1}{4}$ tsp dried mint
1 tbsp chopped parsley or dill,
  to garnish

For the sauce:
1 x 14-oz can of chopped tomatoes
1 tsp sugar
A pinch of turmeric
A pinch of cinnamon
A pinch of cayenne pepper
$\frac{1}{4}$ tsp sea salt
$\frac{1}{4}$ tsp black pepper
$\frac{1}{3}$ cup hot water

Pre-heat the oven to 425°F.

Cut the eggplants in half lengthways, keeping the stem intact. Scoop out the flesh, leaving a $\frac{1}{3}$-inch border. Set the flesh aside for later. Drizzle the eggplant shells generously with olive oil and season generously with salt and pepper. Place in a shallow baking tray, skin-side down, and bake for 30–40 minutes until soft. Check halfway through the cooking time and if the eggplants are looking a little dry, add a bit more olive oil.

Meanwhile, prepare your stuffing. Place the lentils in a medium saucepan, cover with water, and bring to the boil. Reduce the heat and simmer for 12–15 minutes until tender, then drain and place in a bowl.

Heat 2 tablespoons of sunflower oil in the saucepan and fry the onions over a medium heat for 10 minutes, covered. Set aside half of the onions. Add 4 of the garlic cloves to the saucepan and cook for 2 minutes. Add the rice, stock, turmeric, cinnamon, cayenne pepper, and hot water. Season with $\frac{1}{2}$ teaspoon of salt and $\frac{1}{2}$ teaspoon of pepper. Cover and leave to simmer over a low heat for 15 minutes.

Meanwhile, make your sauce. Tip the tomatoes into a saucepan then add the reserved fried onions, along with the sugar, turmeric, cinnamon, cayenne, salt, and pepper. Add the hot water and simmer, covered, for 15 minutes.

To finish making the stuffing, finely dice the eggplant flesh. Heat up 2 tablespoons of sunflower oil in a small frying pan and fry the eggplant with $\frac{1}{4}$ teaspoon of salt for 10 minutes. Add the last clove of garlic and cook for a final minute. Add the lentils and rice to the eggplants, followed by the tomato purée and dried mint. Stir well to combine, then taste and adjust the seasoning.

Turn the oven down to 375°F. Spoon the stuffing into each eggplant half and then spoon the sauce over and around the eggplants. Cover with foil and bake for around 1 hour, by which time the eggplants should be completely soft. Halfway through cooking check the sauce, and if it looks a bit dry then add a few tablespoons more water. Just before serving sprinkle with some parsley or dill.

Serves 4

Rice with lentils, dates, and walnuts
Addas polo

Addas polo is one of life's simple pleasures: a lightly spiced, deeply comforting rice dish cooked with lentils and topped with dried fruit, nuts, and crispy fried onions. Variations of it are eaten throughout the Middle East but the Iranian version uses local dates and walnuts. Filmmaker Behzad Nalbandi shared his own version of the recipe with me on a hot afternoon in his steamy kitchen in Tehran; it is best served with lots of natural yogurt—to balance the sweetness of the dates and raisins—and a Salad Shirazi (page 88).

3/4 cup brown lentils, rinsed
1 3/4 cups white basmati rice
Sea salt
1/2 tsp cumin seeds
1/4 tsp cilantro seeds
Sunflower oil
1 tsp ground cinnamon
1/2 tsp turmeric
1/4 tsp black pepper
1 tbsp butter

For the toppings:
2 medium onions, finely sliced
   into half-moons
2 tbsp all-purpose flour
Sea salt
Sunflower oil
1 tbsp butter
1/4 cup + 2 tbsp raisins
12 Iranian or Medjool dates,
   pitted and roughly chopped
1/2 cup walnuts, roughly chopped
A handful of basil leaves (optional)

Place the lentils in a medium saucepan, cover with water, and bring to the boil. Reduce the heat and simmer for around 20 minutes, or until they are cooked through but still firm to the touch. Drain and place in a bowl.

Meanwhile, rinse and parboil your rice, following the method on page 136.

Dry fry the cumin and cilantro seeds over a medium heat for a minute or two, then grind them with a pestle and mortar or a spice grinder. Place the cooked rice and lentils in a large mixing bowl and add 1 tablespoon of sunflower oil, the cumin, cilantro, cinnamon, turmeric, 1/4 teaspoon of pepper, and 1/2 teaspoon of salt. Gently fold the mixture together, taking care not to break the rice grains.

Heat 1 tablespoon of sunflower oil in a large nonstick saucepan with a tight-fitting lid. Transfer your rice into the pan and follow the method on page 136 to cook the rice.

Meanwhile, prepare your toppings. Sprinkle the sliced onions with the flour and a generous pinch of salt and mix well. Heat a few tablespoons of oil in a large frying pan. When the oil is very hot, add your onions (in batches) and fry them on a medium-high heat for about 6–8 minutes, or until they are golden brown and crunchy. Place the onions on some paper towels to soak up the excess oil and sprinkle over a little more salt.

When the rice is cooked, melt the butter for the toppings in a small frying pan and add the raisins, dates, and walnuts. Sauté for 2 minutes.

To serve, spoon the raisins, dates, and walnuts over the rice and top with the crunchy onions. Scatter with a handful of basil leaves, if you like, and serve immediately.

Serves 4

Garlicky beans with dill and egg
Baghalee ghatogh

This is the ultimate comfort food for my family, perhaps our equivalent of beans on toast. In Iran, we'll often make it with all the ingredients— the fresh beans, dill, garlic, eggs, and rice—taken straight from my grandparents' farm, which adds to the homey feel. Traditionally the beans are first skinned and then split before cooking, so every harvest season, my aunts spread a large cloth on the kitchen floor and sit cross-legged on it, meticulously peeling the skin off each bean. Whenever my mum travels to Iran, she still brings back massive bags of these dried split beans with her, a culinary token of my aunties' labor of love.

Traditionally, Baghalee ghatogh is served with rice, but it goes equally well with crusty bread. For an authentic Gilaki touch, serve it with sweet Iranian pickled garlic on the side, which you should be able to track down in Iranian or Middle Eastern stores.

1¼ cups lima or cannellini beans (soaked for 8 hours or overnight)
¼ tsp turmeric
3 garlic cloves, crushed
3 tbsp finely chopped dill
1 tsp sea salt
Black pepper
2 tbsp extra-virgin olive oil
1¼ cups hot water
2 medium eggs

Rinse the beans in cold water and then place them in a large saucepan with a lid. Pour in enough cold water to cover the beans by at least 2 inches and bring to the boil. Turn down the heat, place the lid on the pot, and leave to simmer for 45 minutes.

Add the turmeric, garlic, dill, salt, and a generous grind of pepper, along with the olive oil and the hot water. Stir well, cover, and leave to cook for 30 minutes. Depending on the age or quality of the beans, they may need a touch more water, so keep an eye on them as they cook.

Crack two eggs into the stew, place the lid on the pan, and leave to cook for 1 minute undisturbed. Run a wooden spoon through each yolk twice (in a cross shape—horizontally and then vertically) so you just break them. Don't mix too much as you want the egg to be in chunks in the final dish, rather than scrambled. Cover and cook for a final few minutes to set the eggs. Check the seasoning, then serve.

Serves 4

Gilaki herb stew
Torsh-e tareh

In northern Iranian cities, it is common to see street sellers crouched by the side of the road, selling large bunches of herbs, freshly harvested and brought in from their farms that day. Iranians buy their herbs by the pound and use them to cook simple yet elegant green stews like this, which are bursting with flavor and make you feel very virtuous, packed as they are with antioxidants and nutrients. This can be served as a side dish or as a vegetarian main with some white rice, or you could add a side dish of some salted or smoked fish, which is how it is usually eaten in Iran.

10 oz spinach
1 medium bunch cilantro
1 medium bunch parsley
1 small bunch dill
4 garlic cloves, crushed
1 tsp turmeric
1¾ cups water
1½ tbsp cornflour mixed to
   a paste with 2 tbsp water

Juice of ½ lemon (plus a few
   extra squeezes, to taste)
2 tbsp extra-virgin olive oil
1 tsp sea salt
½ tsp black pepper
2 medium eggs
Scant tbsp butter

Finely chop the spinach and herbs. For ease and speed you can do this in a food processor. Place all the greens in a saucepan and add the garlic, turmeric, and water. Stir well, cover, and cook for 15 minutes over a low heat.

Add the cornflour paste, lemon juice, olive oil, salt, and pepper. Turn up the heat and cook for 5 minutes with the lid off so that the sauce thickens.

Crack your eggs into the greens. Let them cook for 1 minute without touching them. Run a wooden spoon through each yolk twice (in a cross shape—horizontally and then vertically) so you just break them. Don't mix too much as you want the egg to be in chunks in the final dish, rather than scrambled.

Place the lid on until the eggs are cooked. Take the stew off the heat and stir through the butter to finish. Taste and adjust the seasoning. Traditionally this is a very sour dish so if you like, do feel free to add a few extra squeezes of lemon juice.

Serves 4

Bandari fishcakes with a tamarind and date sauce
Kuku-ye mahi

These fragrant fishcakes are packed full of fresh herbs and fluffy mash, making them soft and pillowy on the inside with a wonderfully crisp crust. They are the result of a morning spent cooking with Goli Heydari, an exuberant primary school teacher from Bandar Abbas. Fish is part of the staple diet in southern Iran and, as Goli showed me, these spicy little parcels are a delicious way to spruce up any cheap white fish. The sweet and spicy tamarind and date sauce adds a lovely piquancy here, and is fun to present in separate little bowls for dunking. Serve the fishcakes with a crisp salad.

2 medium (²/₃ lb) potatoes, peeled and roughly diced
Sea salt and black pepper
¹/₂ lb white fish fillet (such as cod, haddock, or pollock), skinless and boneless, chopped into ¹/₄-inch dice
¹/₄ tsp cumin seeds
1 medium bunch cilantro, finely chopped
1 small bunch parsley, finely chopped, plus extra to garnish
1 tsp dried fenugreek leaf (see page 24)
2 garlic cloves, crushed
A pinch of cayenne pepper
¹/₄ tsp turmeric
Zest of ¹/₂ unwaxed lemon
1 medium egg
All-purpose flour, for dusting
3 tbsp sunflower olive oil

For the tamarind and date sauce:
2 oz tamarind pulp (see page 28), soaked in ¹/₂ cup freshly boiled water for 10 minutes
¹/₂ cup Iranian or Medjool dates, pitted and roughly chopped
1 tbsp light brown sugar
A pinch of cayenne pepper
A pinch of cinnamon
Sea salt
¹/₂ cup + 3 tbsp hot water

Put the potatoes into a large pan and cover with cold water. Add a generous pinch of salt and bring to the boil, then turn down the heat and simmer until tender. Drain, mash the potatoes with a fork or potato masher, and place them in a large mixing bowl.

Add the fish to the potatoes. Dry fry the cumin seeds in a small pan for a minute or so, until their aroma is released. Grind the seeds with a pestle and mortar or a spice grinder and then add them to the bowl, along with the fresh herbs, the fenugreek leaf, garlic, cayenne, turmeric, lemon zest, egg, 1¹/₄ teaspoons of salt, and ¹/₄ teaspoon of pepper.

Using your hands, mix well, then mold into eight round patties. Dust with a little flour and place on a plate, then cover with plastic wrap and chill.

To make your sauce, meanwhile, place the tamarind and its soaking liquid, the dates, brown sugar, cayenne, cinnamon, and a pinch of salt in a small saucepan. Add the hot water and cook for 10 minutes over a low heat until the dates are very soft.

Take the sauce off the heat and sieve into a bowl, using the back of a spoon to rub as much of it through as you can.

To finish the fishcakes, heat the oil in a frying pan and cook the fishcakes on a medium-high heat for 6–8 minutes, turning every few minutes, until golden brown and well crusted. Garnish with parsley, and serve with the sauce in separate bowls, for everyone to dip into.

Serves 4

Grilled mackerel with a spicy pomegranate salsa

In southern Iran, they like it hot; this spicy cilantro and pomegranate salsa pays homage to that part of the country where all the dishes deliver a hefty chile kick. Mackerel is a great fish for serving with a tart and spicy salsa like this, as it always benefits from the addition of something sharp to cut through its strong, oily flavor. I like to serve this with nutty brown rice or some bulgur wheat on the side, for texture.

4 mackerel fillets

For the salsa:
¼ small red onion
½ small red chile, deseeded and finely chopped
Juice of 1 lime

3 tbsp chopped cilantro
3 tbsp parsley, chopped
3 tbsp mint, finely chopped
2 tbsp extra-virgin olive oil
Seeds of 1 pomegranate
Sea salt and black pepper

To make the salsa, slice the red onion very finely into half-moon shapes. Place in a small bowl, mix in the chile and lime juice, and leave to marinate for 15 minutes, to remove some of the red onion's pungency.

Pre-heat the grill to medium-high.

Add the fresh herbs, olive oil, and pomegranate seeds to the onion, season with salt and pepper, and mix well, then set the salsa aside.

Grill the mackerel fillets skin side down for 4–5 minutes until the skin has gone crispy and the fish is firm to the touch. Transfer, skin side up, to a warm plate and spoon over the salsa just before serving.

Serves 4

Mixed herb rice
with baked salmon
Sabzi polo baa mahi

Traditionally served as the first meal of the Iranian New Year, the fresh herbs in this dish symbolize rebirth and renewal. This recipe came out of an afternoon I spent cooking with the Anglo-Iranian rapper Reveal Poison, who made his unique version using soy sauce and cayenne. He explained that he liked the dish so much that he would eat it once a week, and we laughed at the idea that this was the Iranian equivalent of eating Christmas dinner every Saturday.

Sabzi polo can be served with any grilled, baked, or fried fish but as the rice is the star of the show here, be sure to keep the fish simple and don't overpower it with flavors. Serve with plenty of natural yogurt and a salad.

4 salmon fillets

For the mixed herb rice:
1¾ cups white basmati rice
Sea salt
A pinch of saffron strands
A pinch of sugar
2 tbsp freshly boiled water
1 small bunch parsley,
    finely chopped
1 small bunch cilantro,
    finely chopped
2 tbsp dill, finely chopped

2 tbsp chives, finely chopped
1 garlic clove, crushed
Sunflower oil
2 tbsp butter

For the marinade:
2 garlic cloves, minced
¼ cup dark soy sauce
Juice of 1 lemon
3 tbsp extra-virgin olive oil
A pinch of cayenne pepper
    (optional)

To make the marinade, combine the garlic, soy sauce, lemon juice, olive oil, and cayenne pepper in a deep bowl. Add the salmon, turn to coat well, cover with plastic wrap, and leave to marinate in the fridge for at least 30 minutes.

Rinse and parboil the rice and prepare the saffron liquid, following the method on page 136.

Very carefully, fold the rice, chopped herbs, garlic clove, and 1 tablespoon of sunflower oil together, being careful not to break the rice grains.

Pre-heat the oven to 400°F. Place a 8-inch-wide nonstick saucepan with snug-fitting lid over a medium heat. Melt 1 tablespoon butter with 2 tablespoons of sunflower oil. Add 1 tablespoon of the saffron liquid and season with a pinch of salt. Once the fat is hot, sprinkle a thin layer of rice over the bottom and firmly press it down to line the base of the pan. Using a large spoon, gently layer the rest of the rice on top, building it up into a pyramid shape. Using the handle of a wooden spoon, make four holes in the rice. Dot the remaining butter into these and then pour over the rest of the saffron liquid.

Place a clean tea towel or four paper towels on top of the pan and fit the lid on tightly. Tuck in the edges of the tea towel, or trim the paper towels to fit, so they won't catch fire. Cook for 5 minutes over a medium heat, followed by 15 minutes over a very low heat. Take the rice off the heat and leave to sit for a few minutes. Do not be tempted to sneak a peek while it is cooking as this will disturb the steaming process.

When the rice has been cooking for 10 minutes, place the salmon on a baking tray, and bake skin-side up for 10–15 minutes or until the salmon is cooked to your liking.

Once the rice has cooked, fill the sink with an inch of cold water and place the saucepan—with the lid still tightly on it—in the water. This will produce a rush of steam that should loosen the base of the rice. Remove the lid, place a large plate on top of the pan, and quickly turn the rice over. Present the herbed rice with the fish and serve immediately.

Serves 4

Lemon and saffron baked sea bass
Mahi baa zafaron

Across the Middle East, Iranians are famed for their hospitality—this is a nation that loves to entertain, and there is generally enough food to feed at least twice the number of people expected. In Tehran, I helped Nusratalla Sainee, a 73-year-old retired businessman and consummate dinner party host, prepare this baked fish dish; it is his favorite centerpiece when cooking for large groups of friends, accompanied by a platter of beautifully charred vegetables. This also goes wonderfully well with a simple green salad and some Mixed herb rice (previous page) or Persian rice (page 136). Ask your fishmonger for a fish of this size, or alternatively use smaller fish and divide the marinade between them.

¼ tsp saffron strands
A pinch of sugar
2 tbsp freshly boiled water
Extra-virgin olive oil
Sea salt and black pepper
1 large sea bass (about 2 lbs), cleaned and gutted
1 tbsp lemon juice
Zest of ½ unwaxed lemon
½ garlic clove, crushed
¼ tsp sumac
4 bay leaves
A pinch of sumac, to garnish

Make a saffron liquid by grinding the saffron strands with a pinch of sugar using a pestle and mortar. Add the boiled water and leave to steep for 5 minutes.

Line a baking tray with some parchment paper. Lightly grease with a drizzle of olive oil and place the fish on the tray. Using a sharp knife, cut three or four diagonal slashes into each side of the sea bass, almost down to the bone. Season the inside and outside of the fish with salt and pepper.

In a bowl, combine the lemon juice and zest, 3 tablespoons of olive oil, garlic, sumac, and saffron liquid. Rub some of the marinade into the slashes and smear the rest inside the cavity and over the fish.

Place the bay leaves inside the fish and leave to marinate for 15 minutes. Meanwhile, pre-heat the oven to 400°F.

Bake the fish for 20–25 minutes, until it is just cooked through (check by using the tip of a knife to peel the skin away and peek inside at the flesh; it should be white and firm and beginning to flake).

Just before serving, remove the bay leaves and sprinkle with a pinch of sumac and a drizzle of olive oil.

Serves 2

Whole baked fish stuffed with walnuts and pomegranates
Mahi shekampor

Iran's second biggest river, the Sefid Rud, runs from the Alborz mountains all the way to the Caspian Sea, passing through my family's home town—Astaneh-e Ashrafieh—on its way. It used to be full of a prized fish called the Caspian kutum ("mahi sefid"), which my grandmother would stuff with herbs, sour plum molasses, and ground walnuts, and cook for us on special occasions.

These days, a deadly combination of overfishing and pollution means that stocks of kutum are sadly depleted, but the flavors of my grandmother's recipe work just as well with sea bass, sea bream, or any similar firm white fish, as long as it's big—the lengthy cooking time enables the flavors of the stuffing to blend together.

Serve with thin slices of potato, lightly drizzled with olive oil and salt and baked in the oven until soft, and a salad of seasonal green leaves.

Extra-virgin olive oil
¼ cup walnuts
1 small garlic clove, crushed
2 tbsp pomegranate molasses
3 tbsp mint, finely chopped
A small handful of basil, finely chopped
A pinch of golpar (optional)
1 large sea bass
  or sea bream (about 2 lb), cleaned and gutted
Sea salt and black pepper
4 sturdy wooden toothpicks
  or cocktail sticks

Pre-heat the oven to 400°F. Line a baking tray with some parchment paper, then lightly grease it with a drizzle of olive oil.

To make the stuffing, grind the walnuts with a pestle and mortar until you have a smooth paste. Add the garlic, pomegranate molasses, herbs, golpar (if you are using it), a pinch of salt, and a generous grind of pepper.

Place the fish on the lined baking tray, rub a couple of tablespoons of olive oil over it, and then season, inside and out, with salt and pepper.

Pack the stuffing inside the fish then secure with some cocktail sticks or toothpicks placed an inch apart.

Bake the fish in the oven for about 20–25 minutes until it is cooked (check by using the tip of a knife to peel the skin away and peak inside at the flesh; it should be white and firm and beginning to flake). Serve immediately.

Serves 2

Shrimp, cilantro, and tamarind stew
Ghaleyeh maygoo

This sour and spicy stew is one of the hallmarks of southern Iranian cuisine, which is famous for its judicious use of seafood and pungent Indian spices. The holy trinity of southern Iranian cooking—heaps of cilantro, as well as fenugreek and tamarind—are slowly simmered together here to create a bold and aromatic sauce with plenty of kick. For ease and speed I use a food processor to blitz the cilantro but if you do it by hand, try and chop it as finely as possible. Serve with rice and a crisp green salad.

1 oz of tamarind (see page 28)
¼ cup freshly boiled water
3 tbsp sunflower oil
1 medium onion, finely chopped
4 garlic cloves, crushed
2 large bunches cilantro, very finely chopped
¼ tsp cumin seeds
¼ tsp cilantro seeds
½ tsp turmeric
¼ tsp cayenne pepper

2 tsp dried fenugreek leaf (see page 24)
1 tbsp cornflour, mixed to a paste with 2 tbsp cold water
2 tbsp tomato purée
1 tsp sugar
2 cups cold water
1 tsp sea salt
1 tsp black pepper
14 oz shelled raw shrimp

Place the tamarind in a bowl, pour on 3 tablespoons of boiling water, and leave to soak for 10 minutes.

Heat the oil in a large saucepan and fry the onion over a low heat for 10 minutes until soft. Add the garlic and cilantro and then fry for another 10 minutes.

Lightly toast the cumin and cilantro seeds in a small pan over a low heat for a few minutes. Transfer to a spice grinder or a pestle and mortar and grind to a powder. Add to the saucepan, along with the turmeric, cayenne, fenugreek, and cornflour paste and cook for 2–3 minutes.

Push the tamarind through a sieve, pressing with the back of a spoon to get as much pulp as you can. Add the tamarind paste to the saucepan, along with the tomato purée, sugar, water, salt, and pepper. Cover and simmer for 30 minutes over a low heat, stirring occasionally to make sure the stew doesn't stick.

Add the shrimp and cook for 2 minutes or until they have changed color to a pale pink. Taste and adjust the seasoning, then serve immediately.

Serves 4

Lime and saffron chicken kebabs
Jujeh kabob

At least half a dozen different kabobi restaurants crowd into every neighborhood in Iran, and on offer at every one is a version of Jujeh kabob— it's a dish that people all over the country find irresistible. My home-cooked version features succulent, tender chicken cooked in the oven, rather than barbecued on skewers, so you can make it all year round, finishing the chicken under a hot grill to crisp up the skin.

The most important thing here is to marinate the meat for as long as you can, to allow the finger-licking flavors of citrus and saffron to really soak into the chicken. Serve with a pile of warm Persian flatbread (page 60) or some Persian rice (page 136).

1/4 tsp saffron strands
A pinch of sugar
2 tbsp freshly boiled water
8 chicken thighs and drumsticks, bone-in
1/4 tsp turmeric
1 medium onion, finely grated
1 2/3 cup natural yogurt
Juice of 2 limes
3 tbsp extra-virgin olive oil
2 tsp sea salt
1 tsp black pepper
1 tbsp butter, melted
Sumac, for dusting

For the yogurt sauce:
3/4 cup Greek yogurt
1/2 garlic clove, crushed
1 tbsp extra-virgin olive oil
1/2 tsp dried mint
Sea salt and black pepper

To serve:
4 tomatoes, halved
A plate of mixed fresh herbs, such as basil, mint, chives, tarragon, and spring onion

Make a saffron liquid by grinding the saffron strands with a pinch of sugar using a pestle and mortar and then adding the boiled water. Leave to steep for 5 minutes.

With a knife, slash each chicken thigh and drumstick a few times, cutting diagonally, almost to the bone. Mix the saffron liquid, turmeric, onion, yogurt, lime juice, olive oil, salt, and pepper in a large mixing bowl. Add the chicken and mix well to coat with the marinade. Cover with plastic wrap and marinate in the fridge for 3–6 hours, stirring every few hours to make sure every piece of meat is well coated.

Pre-heat the oven to 375°F. In a roasting pan, spread out the chicken pieces skin-side up and cook for around 45 minutes or until the meat is cooked through and the juices run clear. Turn the chicken every 10 minutes so it cooks evenly on both sides.

Meanwhile, heat the grill to high. Grill the tomatoes for about 5–6 minutes, turning frequently, until they are cooked through. Wrap in foil to keep warm until your chicken is ready.

Whisk all the ingredients for the yogurt sauce together and season with some salt and pepper to taste. Set aside.

Move the chicken pieces to a grill rack, skin side up, and pour the melted butter over them. Place under the grill for a final few minutes until the chicken skin is crispy and slightly blackened. Transfer to a serving plate and sprinkle liberally with sumac. Leave to rest for a few minutes before serving with the tomatoes, yogurt sauce, and fresh herbs on the side.

Serves 4

Apricot and prune chicken stew

Aloo mosamaa

This golden, saffron-infused chicken stew is a regional speciality from northern Iran. Its incredible depth of flavor comes from slow cooking the caramelized onions, so don't rush this bit and you will be rewarded with a wonderfully rich and sticky sauce. I would recommend using the widely available soft, sweet, pitted prunes for this recipe, as opposed to the small, dry, salted ones that you sometimes find in Middle Eastern stores. Serve with rice and a green salad.

Sunflower oil
3 medium onions, finely chopped
$^3/_4$ tsp cumin seeds
$^3/_4$ tsp cilantro seeds
$1^3/_4$ lb chicken thighs, boneless, skinless
$1^1/_2$ tsp ground cinnamon
$1^1/_2$ tsp turmeric
1 tsp sea salt

$^1/_2$ tsp black pepper
2 cups good-quality chicken stock
16 dried apricots
16 prunes
$^1/_4$ tsp saffron strands
A pinch of sugar
2 tbsp freshly boiled water
2 tbsp lemon juice

Heat 3 tablespoons of oil in a large saucepan with a lid and gently fry the onions over a low heat, stirring occasionally, until golden brown and caramelized (around 25 minutes).

Meanwhile, toast the cumin and cilantro seeds in a dry frying pan for a minute or two and then grind them into a fine powder with a pestle and mortar or spice grinder.

Once the onions are ready, add the chicken thighs to the saucepan, along with the ground cumin and cilantro, the cinnamon, turmeric, salt, and pepper. Cook with the lid off over a high heat for a few minutes until the chicken is sealed on all sides and then add the stock. Cover and cook over a low to medium heat for 40 minutes.

Meanwhile, heat a tablespoon of oil in a frying pan and lightly fry the apricots and prunes for 2–3 minutes until they start to plump up.

Grind the saffron with a pinch of sugar in the pestle and mortar and then transfer to a cup and leave to steep in the boiled water for 2 minutes.

When the chicken is ready, add the fried fruit, along with the lemon juice and the saffron liquid. Cook for a final 5–10 minutes with the lid off, until the sauce has thickened to your liking. Adjust the seasoning with a touch more salt, pepper, or lemon juice.

Serves 4

Chicken stew with spinach and prunes
Aloo esfinaj

This stew was inspired by a glorious afternoon's cooking in Rasht with pharmacist Sima Mohamadzahdeh, who likes to pot-roast a whole chicken when entertaining guests, presenting it on a bed of spinach and prune sauce. My version of her masterpiece involves poaching flavorful chicken thigh pieces with some warming spices before cooking them in the luscious green sauce. This khoresht is traditionally made with the juice of Seville oranges (narenj), which give a subtle, sweet and sour hint to the chicken and bring out the earthy notes of the spinach. Since these are not widely available here, ordinary oranges combined with lime juice provide an intense, tangy flavor of their own. Serve with rice and a green salad.

Sunflower oil
2 medium onions, finely chopped
2 garlic cloves, crushed
8 chicken thighs, bone-in, skinless
¾ cup good-quality chicken stock
1 tsp turmeric
⅛ tsp ground cinnamon
Sea salt and black pepper
½ tsp saffron strands

A pinch of sugar
2 tbsp freshly boiled water
28 oz spinach, roughly chopped
Juice of 1 lime
Juice of 1 orange
Pared zest of ½ orange, sliced into thin strips
¾ cup (5 oz) prunes
1½ tbsp sliced almonds, to garnish

Heat 3 tablespoons of oil in a large casserole pot and fry the onions over a low heat for 25 minutes, until they are soft and beginning to caramelize. Add the garlic and fry for another 2 minutes.

Turn up the heat and add the chicken. Cook for a few minutes to brown the chicken on all sides. Lower the heat, then add the stock, turmeric, cinnamon, a teaspoon of salt, and ½ teaspoon of black pepper. Cover with a lid and cook for 35 minutes.

Meanwhile, make a saffron liquid by grinding the saffron strands with a pinch of sugar using a pestle and mortar and then adding the boiled water. Leave to steep.

In a large pot or wok, cook the spinach over a high heat until it has wilted and then place in a colander to drain. You'll probably have to do this in a few batches, unless you have an extremely large pot. Let the spinach cool and then squeeze it dry with your hands. Roughly chop and set aside.

After the chicken has been cooking for 35 minutes, add the chopped spinach and the lime and orange juice, along with the orange zest and saffron liquid. Place a lid on the pot and leave to simmer for 10 minutes.

Fry the prunes in 1 tablespoon of oil until they just start to plump up and caramelize. Add them to the stew and cook for a final 5 minutes. Taste and adjust the seasoning, adding more salt and pepper to your preference.

Toast some sliced almonds in a small pan over a low heat for 1 minute until they start to go a golden brown color. Sprinkle the toasted nuts onto the stew just before serving.

Serves 4

Chicken with walnuts and pomegranates
Fesenjoon

This rich and incredibly moreish stew has just three key ingredients, which come together to create a truly sumptuous dish. Fesenjoon is one of the shahs of Persian cuisine and a dish that is often made for special occasions such as weddings. Don't be put off by the time it needs on the stovetop. It couldn't be simpler to make, and once everything is cooking you won't need to do anything other than let it bubble gently in the background.

The longer you leave the walnuts to cook, the more flavorsome the final stew will be, so feel free to let it simmer away before you add the chicken. Be sure to use fresh walnuts, as old ones can make the dish taste bitter.

Serve with white rice, a Salad Shirazi (page 88) and some crunchy radishes on the side. In place of chicken, you could use duck or butternut squash. I often make a delicious vegetarian version with eggplants, which I've included opposite.

2$^1/_2$ cups walnuts (the fresher the better)
5 cups cold water
6 tbsp pomegranate molasses
1 tbsp tomato purée
$^1/_4$ tsp ground cinnamon
2 tbsp sugar
2 tsp sea salt
1 tsp black pepper
$^1/_4$ tsp golpar (optional)
1$^3/_4$ lb chicken thighs, bone-in, skinless
A handful of pomegranate seeds, to garnish

In a food processor, grind the walnuts until they are extremely fine and have the consistency of a smooth paste. Place the ground nuts in a large casserole pot with 4 cups of water and mix well. Bring to the boil and cook on a high heat for 5 minutes, then reduce the heat. Simmer for 1 hour, partially covered, stirring occasionally to stop the walnuts sticking.

Add the remaining cup of water, give the sauce a good stir, then stick the lid back on and leave to simmer for another hour. If the sauce starts looking dry, add some more cold water. You are aiming for a thick, porridge-like consistency.

The sauce should now have thickened and darkened in color. Add the pomegranate molasses, tomato purée, cinnamon, sugar, salt and pepper, and golpar (if you have some) and stir well. Add the chicken pieces, place the lid on the pot, and continue to cook over a low heat for 45 minutes, until the chicken is cooked and the sauce is a glossy, dark chocolate color.

Taste the sauce for seasoning and adjust to your preference: to make it a bit sweeter add more sugar, or pomegranate molasses to make it sourer. Cook for a final 10 minutes with the lid off so the sauce thickens around the meat. Sprinkle with a handful of pomegranate seeds before serving.

Serves 4

Eggplant fesenjoon

Follow the recipe above, substituting the chicken with thick slices of grilled eggplant. While the walnut sauce is cooking, take two eggplants and slice them lengthways in half and then into quarters. Brush the slices with a little olive oil and sprinkle generously with salt.

Heat the grill to medium. Place the eggplants under the grill for about 10 minutes, turning once until they are cooked on both sides. Gently add the eggplants to the stew just before serving to warm them up. Take care not to mix them too much when they are in the pot, as they will disintegrate.

Barberry and saffron rice with chicken

Zereshk polo baa morgh

This shimmering gold and crimson rice dish is an Iranian household staple and one of the most common meals you will eat in Iran. I am indebted here to Faezeh Khorosani, a vivacious project manager who invited me to cook it with her at her home in Tehran, and showed me a great trick for poaching the chicken with the spices first, before lightly sautéing it with the barberries and butter to caramelize the flavors. The result is beautifully tender and buttery chicken with a rich stock you can use to pour over the saffron-infused rice. This goes perfectly with a Salad Shirazi (page 88) and some thick natural yogurt.

1³/₄ cups white basmati rice
³/₄ tsp saffron strands
A pinch of sugar
5 tbsp freshly boiled water
Sunflower oil
1 medium onion, finely chopped
1³/₄ lb chicken thighs, boneless, skinless
¹/₂ tsp turmeric

¹/₂ tsp ground cinnamon
1¹/₄ cups good-quality chicken stock
2 bay leaves
2 tsp fresh lemon juice
Sea salt and black pepper
3 tbsp butter
¹/₃ cup barberries, rinsed
1¹/₂ tbsp granulated sugar

To parboil the rice and prepare the saffron liquid, follow the method on page 136 (adding 5 tablespoons of water to the saffron strands).

In a large saucepan, heat 2 tablespoons of sunflower oil, add the onion, and fry for 10 minutes until soft.

Cut the chicken thighs into bite-sized chunks and add them to the saucepan, along with the turmeric, cinnamon, stock, bay leaves, and the lemon juice. Season with a teaspoon of salt and ¹/₂ teaspoon of pepper, cover, and poach the chicken over a low heat for 45 minutes.

When the chicken has been cooking for 20 minutes, finish cooking your rice in a 8-inch nonstick saucepan (one with a snug-fitting lid). Gently spoon the rice into the pan so that it doesn't all squash down on itself and there is room for the grains to separate. Using the handle of a wooden spoon, create four holes in the rice and fill these with 1 tablespoon butter, broken into four knobs.

Drizzle over 2 tablespoons of the saffron liquid and then place a clean tea towel or four paper towels on top of the pan and fit the lid on tightly, so that no steam can escape. Tuck in the edges of the tea towel, or trim the edges of the paper towels to fit, so they won't catch fire. Cook the rice for 5 minutes over a medium-high heat and then turn the heat down to low and cook for 15 minutes more. Take the rice off the heat and leave to stand for 5 minutes.

When the rice is cooked, remove 1 bowlful of rice from the pan and add 1 tablespoon of the remaining saffron liquid to it. Stir until all the rice in the bowl turns a bright yellow color.

Put a large frying pan over a low heat and melt the remaining butter with 1 tablespoon of sunflower oil. Add the barberries and sugar and stir until the sugar has dissolved. Add the poached chicken with the fried onion (reserve the stock for later) and the rest of the saffron liquid to the frying pan. Sauté with the barberries for a few minutes. Check the seasoning, and add a touch more sugar if you want to.

To serve, spoon the white rice onto your serving plate and top with a few spoonfuls of saffron rice. Place the chicken and barberries on top and finish with a drizzle of the reserved chicken stock.

Serves 4

Roast chicken with pomegranate and za'atar glaze

The dark, sticky juices of my favorite ruby fruit are used here to glaze a humble roast chicken, giving it an opulent wine-red hue and imparting the obligatory Persian sweet and tangy flavor. A good sprinkling of za'atar—a zesty Middle Eastern spice blend—completes the transformation.

Za'atars differ in flavor. I like the Zaytoun brand best. It is sourced from a women's co-operative in the West Bank (I had the pleasure of visiting it some years ago), and the flavor of their dried thyme, sumac, and sesame seed mix is unmatched. I highly recommend finding some, and using it liberally.

This goes beautifully with some Persian rice (page 136) and a Red cabbage, beet, and date salad (page 99).

1 medium chicken (about 3 lbs)
2 tbsp butter
2 tbsp extra-virgin olive oil
1½ tbsp pomegranate molasses

3 tbsp za'atar
1 garlic bulb
½ lemon
Sea salt and black pepper

About 30 minutes before you start cooking, take the chicken and butter out of the fridge to bring them to room temperature.

Pre-heat your oven to 375°F.

Place the chicken in a large roasting pan and massage the butter, olive oil, and pomegranate molasses into its skin. Season generously with salt and pepper, being sure to get plenty inside the chicken's cavity.

Lift the chicken up and sprinkle 1 tablespoon of the za'atar over the skin on its bottom side. Place it down again and sprinkle the remaining 2 tablespoons of za'atar over the skin on top, evenly distributing it.

Peel two cloves of garlic and smash them with the flat blade of a large knife. Place these inside the chicken, along with the lemon. Scatter the remaining unpeeled garlic cloves around the roasting pan.

Place the chicken in the oven and cook for around 1 hour 10 minutes. As oven temperatures can vary, you might want to turn the chicken around halfway through so that it cooks evenly. To check it is done, use the tip of a knife to make a small incision into the thickest part of the meat— if its juices run clear, it is ready. Allow the chicken to rest for 10 minutes before serving.

Serves 4

Lamb meatballs stuffed with barberries and walnuts
Kofte berenji

I was taught how to make these magnificent meatballs by Mehri Sephangekhu, a retired book-keeper from Tehran. We spent a fun afternoon in her bright red tiled kitchen in northern Tehran, squelching the cold ground meat between our fingers before rolling it into orange-sized balls and stuffing them with dried fruit and nuts.

Mehri taught me that the trick to getting a good texture in your meatball is to make sure the meat is very well minced, so get your food processor out to bind all the ingredients together. If you can't get hold of barberries then unsweetened dried cranberries, available from health food shops, will work as a substitute. Serve with bread and a green salad.

For the meatballs:
¹/₄ cup basmati rice
Sea salt
¹/₂ tsp saffron strands
A pinch of sugar
3 tbsp freshly boiled water
1 lb ground lamb
1 small onion, finely chopped
2 garlic cloves, minced
3 tbsp parsley, finely chopped,
   plus 1 tbsp chopped parsley
   to garnish (¹/₄ cup total)
2 tbsp chives, finely chopped
1 tsp dried tarragon
¹/₂ tsp turmeric
¹/₄ tsp cayenne pepper
2 tbsp tomato purée
2 tbsp cornflour

Black pepper
4 prunes
1 tbsp barberries (or unsweetened,
   dried cranberries)
4 walnut halves

For the sauce:
2 tbsp sunflower oil
1 medium onion, finely chopped
1 x 15-oz can of plum tomatoes
1 tbsp brown sugar
A pinch of cayenne pepper
¹/₄ tsp turmeric
¹/₄ tsp ground cinnamon
8 prunes
2 cups hot water
Sea salt and black pepper

Place the rice in a saucepan of water with 1 teaspoon of salt, bring to the boil and cook for 6 minutes. Drain and set aside. Make a saffron liquid by grinding the saffron strands with a pinch of sugar using a pestle and mortar or spice grinder. Add the boiled water and leave to steep.

Blitz the lamb, onion, and garlic in a food processor for a few minutes until the lamb has taken on a sausagemeat consistency. Add the fresh herbs and blitz again. Empty the lamb into a large bowl and add the rice, tarragon, turmeric, cayenne, tomato purée, 1 tablespoon of the saffron liquid, and the cornflour. Season with 1¹/₂ teaspoons of salt and ¹/₂ teaspoon of pepper, then use your hands to knead the mixture for a few minutes, until well combined. Roll the meatballs into four orange-sized balls and set aside.

In a large casserole pot, heat the oil and fry the onion over a medium heat for about 10 minutes, until it is soft. At this point, remove 2 tablespoons of onion and set aside for the stuffing. Add the canned tomatoes to the sauce, along with the sugar, cayenne, turmeric, cinnamon, the remaining 2 tablespoons of saffron liquid, the prunes, and 1 cup hot water. Season well with salt and pepper, then leave to simmer over a low heat while you stuff the meatballs.

To stuff the meatballs, take one in your palm and use the thumb of your opposite hand to press a deep hole into it. Stuff each meatball with a teaspoon of the reserved onion, a prune, a quarter of the barberries, and a walnut half, chopped in two. Reseal the meatball by pinching it in at the top and rolling into a ball again.

Place the filled meatballs in the pot with the sauce, and spoon a bit of it over the meatballs. Put the lid on and simmer for about 50 minutes, checking halfway through to make sure the meatballs haven't stuck to the bottom. Add 1 cup hot water, and spoon more of the sauce over the meatballs. To serve, place one meatball in each bowl and drizzle with the tomato sauce. Finish with a sprinkling of chopped parsley.

Serves 4

Slow-cooked lamb shoulder with dried lime and split peas
Gheimeh

This classic Iranian khoresht is a perfect slow-cooked weekend dish. Its unique flavor comes from the addition of dried limes, which bring a slightly bitter, citrus aroma to the stew. You want the lamb meat on the bone so you get all that lovely marrow flavor; ask your butcher to cut it into small bite-size chunks and to trim off all the fat. And don't skip the topping—the fried potatoes add some much-needed texture and crunch to the final dish.

One final thing: use split peas that are fairly new and haven't been sitting at the back of your cupboard for ages. Old peas can take an incredibly long time to cook and I've been caught out a number of times, having to scoop out the meat then leaving the peas to cook on their own—learn from my mistake. Serve with rice and a green salad.

2 tbsp sunflower oil
2 medium onions, finely chopped
3 garlic cloves, crushed
½ tsp cumin seeds
½ tsp cilantro seeds
1 tsp turmeric
1 tsp ground cinnamon
Black pepper
3 lb lamb shoulder, on the bone, trimmed, cut into 2-inch chunks
1½ cups cold water
3 tbsp tomato purée
½ tsp saffron strands

A pinch of sugar
2 tbsp freshly boiled water
6 dried limes
1 cup yellow split peas, rinsed and soaked for 8 hours or overnight
Sea salt
1 tbsp lemon juice, plus a few spoons more to taste

For the topping:
1 large potato (around ¾ lb)
3 tbsp sunflower oil
Sea salt

Heat the oil in a large saucepan (one with a lid), add the onions and fry over a low heat for 10 minutes until they begin to soften. Add the garlic and fry for a few more minutes.

Dry fry the cumin and cilantro seeds in a small pan over a low heat for a minute or two and then grind them into a fine powder with a pestle and mortar or a spice grinder. Add to the saucepan, along with the turmeric, cinnamon, and ½ teaspoon of pepper.

Add the meat, turn up the heat, and fry until it is browned on all sides. Add the water and tomato purée, put the lid on the pan, and cook over a low heat for 45 minutes.

Prepare a saffron liquid by grinding the strands with a pinch of sugar with the pestle and mortar. Add the boiled water and leave to steep.

After the lamb has been cooking for 45 minutes, pierce each dried lime with a fork a few times and add them to the saucepan along with the yellow split peas. Cook for 40 minutes and then add the saffron liquid, 1½ teaspoons of salt, lemon juice, and a generous grind of black pepper. Squash the dried limes against the side of the saucepan, so their juices are released. Cook for a final 5–10 minutes or until the split peas and lamb are tender.

When the stew is almost ready, prepare your topping. Peel the potato and cut it into matchstick-sized pieces. Sprinkle with salt and then heat the oil in a large frying pan and fry the potato sticks until they are crispy and golden. Transfer the potato sticks to some paper towels to drain, then sprinkle over the stew just before serving.

Serves 4–6

Lamb and mixed herb stew

Ghormeh sabzi

Epitomizing Iran's love affair with green herbs, Ghormeh sabzi is for many people the unofficial national dish— a gorgeous green, slow simmered stew of braised lamb with cilantro, parsley, spinach, chives, and spring onions; tangy dried limes are vital here, giving the stew its uniquely Iranian flavor.

For the best taste, make sure you get the meat on the bone; ask your butcher to cut it into small bite-size chunks and to trim off all the fat. And when you get home, give the lamb another look and trim off any remaining fat, as the dish can release a lot of oil. The amount of herbs that need chopping might look a bit daunting but it shouldn't take more than 10 minutes to do and you can always stick them in a food processor—it won't affect the taste.

This stew tastes even better the next day and freezes well. Serve it with white rice and a green salad.

Sunflower oil
1 medium onion, finely chopped
4 garlic cloves, crushed
3 lb lamb shoulder, on the bone, trimmed, cut into 2-inch chunks
1 tsp turmeric
Sea salt and black pepper
About 2 cups cold water
1 large bunch parsley, finely chopped
1 large bunch cilantro, finely chopped

1 small bunch chives, finely chopped
15 oz spinach, trimmed and finely chopped
2 spring onions, finely chopped
1 x 15-oz can of red kidney beans, rinsed and drained
2 tbsp dried fenugreek leaf (see page 24)
6 dried limes
2 tbsp lemon juice

Heat 2 tablespoons of sunflower oil in a large saucepan (one with a lid). Fry the onion for 10 minutes, until soft, then add the garlic and cook for 2 more minutes. Add the meat, turmeric, and ½ teaspoon of black pepper and brown the meat on all sides. Add enough cold water to cover the meat (around 2 cups), then put the lid on and cook on a medium-low heat for 30 minutes.

Meanwhile, set aside 3 tablespoons parsley and 3 tablespoons cilantro and then place the rest of the herbs, the spinach, and the spring onions in a pan and dry fry over a low heat for 10 minutes to evaporate their water. Stir every so often so the herbs don't stick to the pan. Add 2 tablespoons of sunflower oil to your pan and fry the herbs for a further 10 minutes.

After the lamb has been cooking for 30 minutes, add the cooked greens, red kidney beans, fenugreek, and 1½ teaspoons of salt. Pierce the dried limes a few times with a fork and then add them too. Simmer, with the lid on, for 50 minutes.

Stir through the lemon juice and the reserved parsley and cilantro. Press the dried limes against the side of the pot so they burst and then stir well to mix the flavors together.

Leave to cook for a final 10 minutes and then taste and adjust for seasoning, adding a bit more salt, pepper, or lemon juice, to taste. You can leave the limes in when serving, but you probably won't want to eat them, as they can be very bitter. While I like them, they are something of an acquired taste.

Serves 4–6

Dr. Asaf's juicy lamb kebabs
Chenjeh

My dad lives to eat, and is one of the best cooks I know. Born in Pakistan, he studied to be a doctor in Lahore before moving to Iran in the 1970s as part of an influx of medical professionals from the Indian sub-continent. He fell in love with the culture, the food, and my mother, and the rest— as they say—is history.

Dad loves his meat, and is never happier than when there is a huge plate of barbecued lamb in front of him, which might explain why he and Iran took to each other so well. His special bite-sized kebabs are famous among our family and friends. So this is my ultimate gift to you, the best Iranian kebab recipe you'll find— from my Pakistani dad.

I usually cook these indoors, but if the weather is fine, barbecuing the lamb will give you all those extra-tasty smoky flavors from the coals. Serve with Persian rice (page 136), a Mixed herb platter (page 54) and a bit of Yogurt with cucumber and dill (page 64).

4 tbsp natural yogurt
1 small onion, finely grated
1 garlic clove, crushed
½ tsp oregano
1 tbsp extra-virgin olive oil
¾ tsp sumac, plus extra to garnish
A generous pinch of cayenne pepper
1¼ tsp sea salt
1 tsp black pepper
2 lb lamb neck fillet, trimmed, cut into 2-inch cubes
4 tomatoes, halved
skewers (optional; if wooden, soak them in water for a few hours first)

In a large bowl, mix the yogurt with the onion, garlic, oregano, oil, sumac, cayenne, salt, and pepper. Add the lamb, stir to coat with the marinade, then cover and chill for 2–3 hours, to tenderize the meat and allow the flavors to really come together.

When ready to cook, light the barbecue or heat your grill pan or broiler to high. Thread the kebabs onto skewers or place them on a wire rack if you are cooking them under the broiler. Thread the tomatoes on separate skewers. Cook the tomatoes and lamb for about 5–7 minutes, turning frequently, until the kebabs are cooked through.

Let the meat rest for a few minutes, then sprinkle with sumac before serving.

Serves 4

Rice with lamb, tomatoes and green beans
Loobia polo

As a child, I always got a little kick of excitement in my belly when I arrived home from school to the smell of "Loobia polo" cooking on the stovetop, filling the house with its sweet scent of warming spices. This dish is perfect for a winter weekend when you want something robust and filling to keep you warm. The lamb and the vegetables are cooked separately here, and then added in layers to the parboiled rice before the whole thing is steamed together. The result is Iranian home cooking at its best. Serve with lots of natural yogurt and a green salad.

1²⁄₃ cups white basmati rice
Sea salt
¼ tsp saffron strands
A pinch of sugar
4 tbsp freshly boiled water
3 tbsp sunflower oil
1 medium onion, finely chopped
2 garlic cloves, crushed
1 tsp cumin seeds
1 tsp cilantro seeds
1 tsp turmeric
1 tsp ground cinnamon

¼ tsp allspice
A pinch of cayenne pepper
½ tsp black pepper
14 oz ground lamb
1 x 8-oz can of plum tomatoes
1 medium potato (around ¾ lb),
    peeled and chopped into ½-inch
    dice
¾ cup water
½ lb green beans, cut into thirds
2 tbsp tomato purée

Wash the rice in several changes of cold water until the water runs clear
and then leave it to soak in a large bowl of water for 15 minutes.

Drain the rice and bring a large pot of water to the boil with 2 tablespoons
of salt. (Don't worry about the amount of salt here, the rice has a very short
time to absorb the water and the final result won't be too salty). Add the rice
and cook for 4–5 minutes over a medium heat. Taste to test; it should be
soft on the outside but still firm in the middle. Drain, rinse with tepid water
to stop it cooking any further, and set aside.

Make the saffron liquid by grinding the saffron with a pinch of sugar with a
pestle and mortar and then transfer to a small bowl and leave to steep in the
boiled water.

Heat 2 tablespoons of sunflower oil in a saucepan with a lid and add the
onion. Fry on a medium heat for 10 minutes until soft, then add the garlic
and cook for a further 2 minutes.

Dry fry the cumin and cilantro seeds in a small pan over a medium heat for
a minute or two and then grind them with the pestle and mortar or spice
grinder. Toss into the saucepan with the onions, along with the turmeric,
cinnamon, allspice, cayenne, pepper, and lamb. Cook for 2 minutes to
brown the meat and then add the tomatoes, potato, and water. Cover and
cook on a medium-low heat for 15 minutes.

Add the green beans to the pot, along with the tomato purée, 2 teaspoons
of salt, and 2 tablespoons of the saffron liquid. Cover and cook for a final
10 minutes. The final mixture should be quite dry.

Begin to layer your rice dish: pour 1 tablespoon of sunflower oil in the
bottom of a nonstick saucepan with a snug-fitting lid and place on a
medium heat. Add 1 tablespoon of the saffron liquid, and then a layer of
rice, followed by a layer of the meat, beans, and potatoes. Repeat with the
remaining rice and meat until it is all used up. Spoon over the last bit of
saffron liquid, then place a clean tea towel or four layers of paper towels on
top of the saucepan and put the lid on tightly. Tuck in the edges of the tea
towel, or trim the edges of the paper towels to fit, so they don't catch fire.
Cook over a low heat for 20 minutes.

When the dish is cooked, remove from the heat and leave to stand for
5 minutes before serving.

Serves 4–6

Spiced beef with eggs and spring onions
Vaavishkaa

This rustic dish from the north of Iran was one of my grandfather's favorite meals and, according to my gran, the only thing he knew how to cook. The name, Vaavishkaa, suggests it is of Russian origin, which is unsurprising given the trade activity along the shores of the Caspian Sea over the centuries. Whatever its origins, it is a great dish to make if you want to whip up something quick and easy. The beef is first poached and then lightly fried with tomatoes and spices—perfect for scooping up with some flatbread or serving with fluffy white rice, some natural yogurt, and a crunchy Salad Shirazi (page 88); a few radishes would go down very well too.

1 lb ground beef
1 medium onion, finely chopped
1³⁄₄ cups cold water
1 tsp turmeric
¹⁄₂ tsp black pepper
4 tomatoes
2 tbsp tomato purée

¹⁄₄ tsp cayenne pepper
1 tsp sea salt
2 tbsp sunflower oil
2 medium eggs
2 spring onions, trimmed and finely chopped, to garnish

Place the meat and onions in a saucepan and pour in the cold water. Add the turmeric and pepper and stir well. Place a lid on the pan and simmer for 20 minutes over a low heat.

Meanwhile, skin the tomatoes by scoring the skins with a sharp knife a few times and placing them in a bowl of just boiled water for about a minute. Drain well, then rub off the skin. Cut the tomatoes in half, remove and discard the seeds, then cut into small dice.

Add the diced tomato to the pan, along with the tomato purée, cayenne, and salt, followed by the oil. Simmer with the lid on for another 15 minutes, stirring occasionally, and then cook for 5 minutes with the lid off until the sauce has the consistency of a thick ragu.

Crack the eggs into the pan and leave to set for a minute. Gently run a wooden spoon through the yolks a few times. Don't mix too much, as you want to have chunks of egg in the final dish, not scrambled eggs. Place a lid on until the eggs are set and then taste to adjust the seasoning.

Serve with the spring onions sprinkled on top.

Serves 4

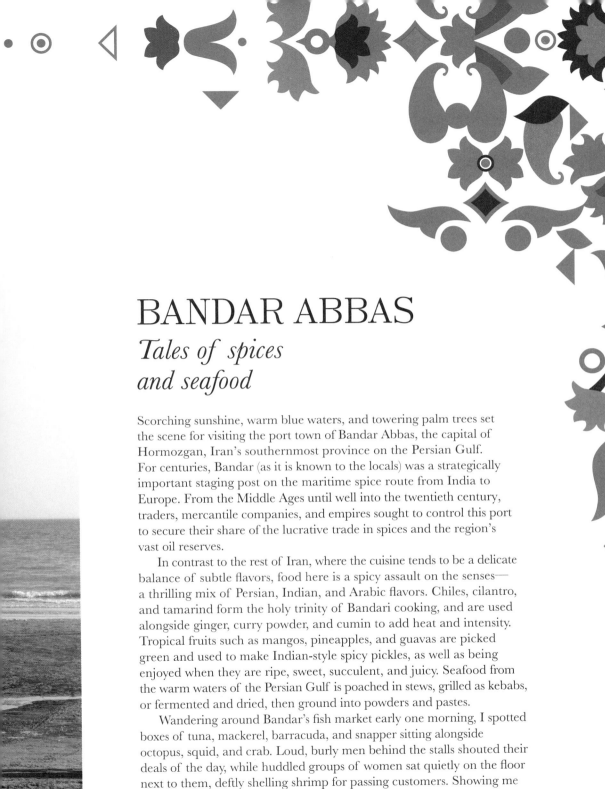

BANDAR ABBAS
*Tales of spices
and seafood*

Scorching sunshine, warm blue waters, and towering palm trees set the scene for visiting the port town of Bandar Abbas, the capital of Hormozgan, Iran's southernmost province on the Persian Gulf. For centuries, Bandar (as it is known to the locals) was a strategically important staging post on the maritime spice route from India to Europe. From the Middle Ages until well into the twentieth century, traders, mercantile companies, and empires sought to control this port to secure their share of the lucrative trade in spices and the region's vast oil reserves.

In contrast to the rest of Iran, where the cuisine tends to be a delicate balance of subtle flavors, food here is a spicy assault on the senses—a thrilling mix of Persian, Indian, and Arabic flavors. Chiles, cilantro, and tamarind form the holy trinity of Bandari cooking, and are used alongside ginger, curry powder, and cumin to add heat and intensity. Tropical fruits such as mangos, pineapples, and guavas are picked green and used to make Indian-style spicy pickles, as well as being enjoyed when they are ripe, sweet, succulent, and juicy. Seafood from the warm waters of the Persian Gulf is poached in stews, grilled as kebabs, or fermented and dried, then ground into powders and pastes.

Wandering around Bandar's fish market early one morning, I spotted boxes of tuna, mackerel, barracuda, and snapper sitting alongside octopus, squid, and crab. Loud, burly men behind the stalls shouted their deals of the day, while huddled groups of women sat quietly on the floor next to them, deftly shelling shrimp for passing customers. Showing me around was Mehrnaz Mehragin, a design student at Hormozgan

University, who explained the market's appeal: "You can find any kind of fish you want here. Hundreds of different types are caught locally and we buy what is available by season."

I bought 2 pounds of shrimp to take to Mehrnaz's house, as we planned to cook one of the province's signature dishes—*Ghaleyeh maygoo* (page 162). On our way out, we spotted a woman sitting on the street corner preparing a local delicacy—wafer-thin crèpes sprinkled with a spice rub made from fermented dried shrimp and crushed, red rock from nearby Hormoz Island. This mineral-rich volcanic dust is added to several local sauces and is said to hold special powers, so I bought a couple of the crèpes to share, then couldn't get past a few bites as the dank smell of the sea filled my nostrils.

Back at Mehrnaz's house, her aunt, Mina Manzaran, put me to work in the kitchen, chopping forests of cilantro to go in our spicy, emerald green stew. We cooked against a backdrop of local music blaring out of the TV and the infectious beats of the djembe drums playing the signature Bandari rhythm. With the food simmering away on the stove, Mina showed me how to make a Bandari dry spice mix with turmeric, cilantro, cumin, ginger, and chile that smells like garam masala, and can be used to marinate fish, season rice, or flavor stews.

Mehrnaz then proceeded to decorate my hand with henna patterns, another nod to the Indian influence that permeates modern Bandar Abbas. It was a touching gesture, but one that presented me with a dilemma once we sat down on the floor to eat the food: how was I going to eat with one hand so I wouldn't ruin the design, which needs an hour

to dry? Faced with a feast of juicy shrimp and steaming rice, accompanied by crunchy pieces of the rice crust known as *tahdig*, and yogurt and mango pickles, I determinedly rose to the challenge.

At the home of musician Ahmad Ravon, a percussionist and rapper of African-Iranian descent, and his wife, Goli Heydari, a local school teacher, I learnt more about the region's history. Ahmad told me that after the Portuguese relinquished control of Hormozgan in the sixteenth century, many of the slaves they had brought with them from East Africa as free men stayed in Iran, keeping their cultural customs alive. A key part of this was playing music at social gatherings, which is why music has remained such an intrinsic part of Bandari life, unlike many areas of Iran where—since the Islamic Revolution of 1979 restricted the playing and performing of popular music—you hardly hear any music in public at all.

Ahmad was just offering to teach me how to play some typical Bandari rhythms when Goli swept in and pulled me into the kitchen to show me her recipe for Bandari fishcakes, flavored with lots of cilantro and parsley (page 155). I asked my hostess what she thinks makes a good cook. "Love and intention," she exclaimed brightly. "If you put the love that is in your heart into the food you make, it will always taste good." Squeezing the mashed potato and fish into little patties with my hands, as Goli got to work on some Mixed herb rice (page 158) and a spicy Salad Bandari (page 88), I suddenly I felt like I was back at school again, desperate to impress the teacher and get a gold star for my fishcake-shaping efforts.

After lunch, Ahmad taught me how to play a local percussion instrument, the *jaleh* (a clay water jug that you hit with your palms), as Goli scuttled around us, pouring tea, serving fruit, and singing harmonies. Ahmad rapped one of his songs—an ode to Bandar Abbas—over our beats.

Rap music, even his kind of local folk-rap, can't be produced or played in public without a permit from Iran's Ministry of Culture and Guidance, but along with many musicians in Iran, Ahmad prefers to remain independent of the state and so chooses not to ask for permission to make his music—hence the emergence of the country's vibrant underground music scene.

I jotted down a list of names of prominent musicians my host suggested I look up and then returned to the *jaleh*, as we played well into the afternoon, enjoying Goli's endless cups of tea and helping ourselves to more fruit whenever our hands got tired.

I felt myself drawn to Bandar, discovering there a different side of Iran—vibrant and colorful and pulsating with life, from the sound of tribal drums emanating from every shopfront to the brightly patterned and sequin-studded clothes of the local women, to the vibrant cuisine.

Another dining partner of mine, trainee architect Aida Jafari, sums up the appeal well: "It is so hot here. Temperatures in the summer soar above 122°F and even in winter it is still 77°F, and I think we inject that heat into every part of our culture—the food, the music and the way people treat each other. Everything about this place is warmer than other places in Iran."

In a small café tucked away off a side street—the kind of unassuming place you could easily walk past—Aida and I shared a a typical Bandari breakfast. As soon as we sat down, we were served black tea, speckled with small dots of ground cardamom and showered with a feast of za'atar-covered *maneesh* (yeasted flatbread the size of my palm); *borek*, a deep-fried filo pastry filled with egg; and *Baalaaloot* (page 42), a supremely elegant dish of sweet vermicelli fried in butter, saffron, cardamom, and sugar, then topped with a fried egg.

"*Baalaaloot* makes me think of my family," Aida revealed. "My mother would always make a big pot of it and we would eat it for breakfast at Eid." It certainly tastes like a festive dish—just the right balance of indulgence and celebration, reminiscent of the kinds of dishes you might eat at an Indian wedding.

Walking along the seafront after our meal, the sun was already so hot at 9 am that I had to reach for my sunscreen. I settled on the rocks, dipping my toes in the clear, blue water, and watched the videos on my phone of Ahmad and me playing the drums the day before. The sounds of the music, the twinkling water and the light, spice-laden breeze filled my senses as I relished the cultural melting pot I had found at the southernmost tip of this majestic country.

DESSERTS

THERE ARE SPECIALIST patisseries in every neighborhood of Iran, selling an assortment of *shirini*, the Farsi term for a sweet baked good. These brightly lit *shirini* stores are a confectioner's dream, smelling of warm vanilla sugar with a slight hint of sour fermenting yeast. Inside, row upon row of glass cabinets display a dazzling selection of cream puffs, saffron pastries, almond biscuits, fruit tarts, nut brittles, pistachio nougat, and sticky baklava, all of which are sold in boxes by the pound. As it is considered impolite to arrive at someone's house empty-handed in Iran, a box of *shirini* is often taken as a gift when visiting family and friends. I secretly revel in this custom and use the excuse of visiting people to indulge my sweet tooth and roam guilt-free across town, finding the best *shirini* stores and filling my bags with the most unusual and indulgent treats.

Saffron, cardamom, cinnamon, nutmeg, and cloves are the dominant spices used in Iranian *shirini*, along with the floral notes of rose water and orange blossom water. Jams and fresh fruits such as strawberries, figs, apricots, dates, sour cherries, and apples are often used to stuff tarts or are layered into cakes, while pistachios, almonds, and walnuts are used whole to add texture and color or ground into a flour.

For all their love of *shirini*, Iranians don't actually have a culture of eating dessert and tend to eat these sweet morsels during the day, alongside their endless cups of tea. Because meals are traditionally finished with just fresh fruit and tea, many of the cakes and tarts served in Iran for special occasions are interpretations of classic Western desserts. The recipes in this chapter reflect this approach, and celebrate the flavors and ingredients of Persian cuisine in familiar Western-style cakes and puddings.

Persian love cake

This enchanting cake reminds me of a Persian garden in the late spring, adorned with the floral scent of rose water and citrus, and decorated with bright green pistachios. If it is not devoured in one sitting, the oil in the ground almond base ensures a moist, densely textured cake that will keep well for a couple of days, covered in foil. A sprinkling of dried rose petals looks ever so pretty for special occasions, but don't worry if you can't get hold of any. It's still a cake to win hearts.

7 oz (1³/₄ stick) unsalted butter
Scant ²/₃ cup superfine sugar
4 medium eggs
12 cardamom pods
³/₄ cup all-purpose flour, sifted
2³/₄ cups ground almonds
Zest and juice of 1 unwaxed lemon
1 tbsp rose water
1 tsp baking powder
A pinch of fine sea salt

For the drizzle topping:
2 tbsp superfine sugar
Juice of ¹/₂ lemon
¹/₂ tbsp rose water

For the icing:
1¹/₄ cups confectioners' sugar
Juice of ³/₄ lemon
2 tsp cold water

To decorate:
2 tsp chopped pistachios
2 tsp dried rose petals (optional)

Pre-heat the oven to 320°F. Grease a 9-inch springform pan and line it with parchment paper.

In a large mixing bowl, cream the butter and sugar together. When the mixture is thoroughly combined, beat in the eggs.

Place the cardamom pods in a mortar and work with a pestle to get the seeds out of the pods. Discard the pods and grind the seeds to a fine powder. Add them to the cake mixture, along with the flour, ground almonds, lemon zest and juice, rose water, baking powder, and salt. Mix well.

Pour the mixture into the cake pan and bake in the oven for 45 minutes. To check if it is ready, stick a fork in the middle of the cake—it should come out dry.

Towards the end of the cooking time, make your drizzle topping. Place the superfine sugar, lemon juice, and rose water in a small pan over a low heat and heat until the sugar melts.

Remove the cake from the oven and place it on a wire rack. Poke holes all over the top of the warm cake and drizzle over the syrup.

When the cake is completely cool, make the icing by combining the confectioners' sugar, lemon juice and a few teaspoons of water until you have a smooth, thick icing. Spoon the icing over the cake and finish with a sprinkling of pistachios and, if you like, rose petals.

Serves 6–8

Chocolate and pistachio torte

This classic, flourless dark chocolate torte has enough depth and richness to satisfy any chocolate lover while being light enough to justify a second helping. That's win-win in my book. Pistachio nuts are prized in Iran and their natural sweetness works wonders with dark chocolate. Here they are ground down to give a nutty and textured base to the torte. To get the cake as fluffy as possible, grind the pistachios as fine as you can and don't overmix the batter, so you keep the air in it.

1 cup shelled unsalted pistachios
6 oz dark chocolate (70%), broken into chunks
5 oz (1¼ stick) unsalted butter
1 tsp vanilla extract

8 medium eggs, separated
¾ cup superfine sugar
4 tsp cocoa powder
¼ tsp fine sea salt
1 tsp confectioners' sugar (optional), for dusting

Grind the pistachios in a food processor until they resemble fine breadcrumbs. Set aside 1 teaspoon for dusting the cake, if you like.

Gently melt the chocolate and butter in a heatproof bowl over a pan of simmering water, stirring occasionally. Remove from the heat and add the vanilla extract. Leave to cool slightly.

Pre-heat the oven to 320°F. Grease a 10-inch springform cake pan and line the base with parchment paper.

Whisk the egg yolks and sugar together using an electric whisk for about 3–4 minutes, until the mixture is pale and fluffy.

In a separate bowl, whisk the egg whites until they form firm peaks.

Carefully stir the chocolate and melted butter into the egg yolks, along with the ground pistachios, cocoa, and salt. Then fold in the egg whites, trying to keep as much air in the mixture as possible.

Gently pour the batter into the lined cake pan and bake for 35–40 minutes until the cake has set on top but is still a little wobbly in the middle.

Transfer to a wire rack and leave to cool, then sprinkle on the reserved pistachios or some confectioners' sugar (or both, if you prefer).

Serves 8–10

Pomegranate and sour cherry sponge cake

Lavish, layered sponge cakes, adorned with colorful fresh fruit and mounds of whipped cream, are an essential part of any birthday or anniversary celebration in Iran. This recipe is a cross between those traditional desserts and a good old Victorian sponge, with sour cherries and pomegranates adding a Persian twist to the British classic. You can find jars of sour cherry jam in most large supermarkets, sometimes labeled Morello cherry jam.

7 oz (1³/₄ stick) unsalted butter, plus extra for greasing
1 cup superfine sugar
4 medium eggs
2 tbsp whole milk
¹/₂ vanilla pod or
   1 tsp vanilla extract
1¹/₂ cups self-rising flour
1 tsp baking powder
Fine sea salt

For the filling:
³/₄ cup heavy cream
1 tbsp lemon juice
1 tbsp superfine sugar
¹/₂ cup + 2 tbsp sour cherry jam
2 tbsp pomegranate seeds

To finish:
Confectioners' sugar
1 tbsp pomegranate seeds

Pre-heat the oven to 375°F. Grease a pair of 8-inch springform cake pans and line the bases with parchment paper.

In an electric mixer with a beater attachment, or in a bowl with a wooden spoon, cream the butter and sugar together until light and fluffy. Beat in the eggs one by one, then stir in the milk. If you are using the vanilla pod, slice it in half lengthways and scrape the seeds into the bowl with the point of a knife. Alternatively, add a teaspoon of vanilla extract.

Sift the flour and baking powder into the batter and add a pinch of salt. Lightly whisk the batter until it is completely smooth.

Divide the cake batter between the two pans and bake for about 20 minutes. The sponges are done when a fork stuck into the middle comes out clean. Turn the cakes out of the pans and leave to cool completely on a wire rack.

To make the creamy part of the filling, whisk the cream with the lemon juice and sugar until it forms soft peaks.

When the cakes have cooled, spread the cream over the bottom of one. Spread the jam over the other cake, followed by the pomegranate seeds. Sandwich the two sponges together.

Dust with a little confectioners' sugar and sprinkle over the pomegranate

Serves 6–8

Yogurt cake
with poached figs

This beautifully light summer pudding is delicious lukewarm or chilled. In Tabriz, in the north-east of Iran, yogurt cakes are popular served with all kinds of refreshing fruit on the side, from pomegranates to peaches. I love the sweet poached figs here, which offset the lemony sharpness of the yogurt perfectly, but you can use whatever seasonal fruit looks good. This cake has a very moist texture, a bit like a soufflé, so don't be surprised if it collapses in on itself a little as it cools.

4 medium eggs, separated
$^{1}/_{2}$ cup + 3 tbsp superfine sugar
1 tsp vanilla extract
1$^{1}/_{2}$ cups Greek yogurt
$^{1}/_{4}$ cup + 2 tbsp all-purpose flour
Zest and juice of $^{1}/_{2}$ unwaxed lemon

For the poached figs:
2 tbsp honey
$^{1}/_{3}$ cup water
1 tsp vanilla extract
3 tbsp sugar
4 ripe figs, sliced in quarters

Pre-heat the oven to 350°F. Grease an 8-inch springform cake pan and line the base with parchment paper.

Beat the egg yolks with the sugar until thick and pale, then beat in the vanilla extract. Add the yogurt, flour, lemon zest, and juice and mix until combined.

In a separate bowl, whisk the egg whites with an electric whisk until they form firm peaks. Very gently fold the whisked egg white into the yogurt mixture with a large spoon, keeping as much air in the batter as possible.

Pour the mixture into the cake pan and bake for 45–50 minutes until firm to the touch and golden on top.

Leave the cake to cool on a wire rack while you prepare your figs. Heat the honey, water, vanilla extract, and sugar in a small saucepan. Add the figs and poach for 5–6 minutes or until the figs have softened but still have their shape.

Transfer the figs and syrup to a serving bowl. When you are ready to eat the cake, cut each person a slice and serve with the poached fruit and syrup spooned over or on the side.

Serves 4–6

Rhubarb and cardamom cheesecake

In ancient Persian Zoroastrian mythology, the first man and woman are said to have emerged from the rhubarb plant. It's a creation story I loved as a child, as it elevated this everyday British plant into something altogether more sophisticated and ethereal.

Rhubarb is used in both savory and sweet dishes in Iran and in this simple bake, the warming spices of ginger and cardamom really make it sing. The cake needs to be chilled for at least 3 hours before serving and tastes even more delicious when left overnight, so this is a great dessert to make in advance.

7 oz gingersnap cookies
2 oz ($^1/_2$ stick) unsalted butter, melted
12 cardamom pods
$^3/_4$ lb rhubarb, cut into 1-inch pieces
$^1/_4$ cup + 1 tbsp superfine sugar
$^1/_4$ cup water

1 lb cream cheese
Zest of 1 unwaxed lemon
1 tsp vanilla extract
1 x 14-oz can of condensed milk
3 medium eggs
2 tbsp cornflour

Pre-heat the oven to 400°F. Line the base of a 9-inch springform cake pan with parchment paper.

Place the cookies in a large plastic food bag and roll with a rolling pin to crush finely, or blitz to fine crumbs in a food processor.

Transfer the cookie crumbs to a bowl, pour over the melted butter, and stir well. Layer the mixture into the base of the lined cake pan, pressing into an even layer. Bake in the pre-heated oven for 10 minutes, then leave to cool to room temperature in the pan.

In a mortar, work the cardamom pods with a pestle to get the seeds out of the pods. Discard the pods and grind the seeds to a fine powder.

Place the rhubarb, sugar, half of the ground cardamom, and $^1/_4$ cup of water in a saucepan. Cook until the rhubarb is soft and tender, around 4–8 minutes. Take off the heat and sieve the rhubarb, keeping the juices. Set the sieved rhubarb aside to cool.

Return the rhubarb juice to the saucepan and cook over a medium heat for 2–3 minutes until reduced to a sticky syrup. Remove from the heat and allow to cool.

Pre-heat the oven to 350°F. For the cheesecake filling, mix together the cream cheese, lemon zest, vanilla extract, condensed milk, and remaining cardamom in a large bowl. Beat in the eggs and the cornflour and then gently fold in two thirds of the cooked rhubarb.

Take the cake pan out of the fridge and pour in the cheesecake filling. Transfer to the oven and bake for around 45 minutes until it is firm to the touch but still slightly wobbly in the middle.

Leave the cheesecake to cool completely before removing it from the pan and spooning over the remaining rhubarb and the syrup as a topping. Transfer to the fridge and leave to chill for at least 3 hours before serving.

Serves 6–8

Poached quince with mascarpone and pistachios

In the Middle Ages, golden quinces were prized in Britain, with quince trees planted all over the country, and in the grounds of royal palaces. Today, they are more famous for being eaten with mince by the owl and the pussycat. But in Iran they are still a popular treat, peeled, sliced, and eaten raw, or cooked down into jams, savory dishes, or desserts. They are available in the UK from late autumn to early spring, at Turkish, Indian, or Middle Eastern stores, and some local farmers' markets. Look for fruit with a deep yellow color and the most intense floral scent.

The poached quinces will keep for several days in the fridge. If you are avoiding dairy you can eat them in just their syrup. They are also nice on top of porridge or with some natural yogurt and granola for breakfast.

3 1/3 cups water
3/4 cup brown sugar
5 cloves, lightly crushed
1/4 tsp ground cinnamon
1 tbsp rose water
2 large quinces, peeled and halved
 with the core removed

For the toppings:
2 tbsp pistachios, roughly chopped
1/4 cup mascarpone or crème fraîche
1 tsp confectioners' sugar
1 tsp freshly squeezed lemon juice

Place the water, sugar, cloves, cinnamon, and rose water in a saucepan and bring to a boil.

Add the quinces and simmer for about 30 minutes until they are quite soft.

Pre-heat the oven to 350°F. Scoop the quinces out of the pan and place them in an ovenproof dish. Return the pan to the stovetop and cook the sauce for a further 5 minutes over a high heat to reduce.

Pour half of the reduced sauce over the quinces, then place them in the oven and cook for about 20 minutes, or until they are very soft to the touch.

Meanwhile, prepare the toppings. Lightly toast the chopped pistachios by dry frying them in a small pan for a few minutes. In a small bowl, mix the mascarpone or crème fraîche with the confectioners' sugar and lemon juice.

Arrange the quinces on a serving plate and spoon over a few tablespoons of the poaching sauce, a dollop of cream, and a sprinkling of toasted nuts.

Serves 4

Apricot and pistachio tart with orange blossom cream

Apricots in Iran are sheer perfection—succulent, juicy, and best eaten straight off the trees in the height of summer. It is harder to get your hands on great apricots here, so I use canned ones for this Persian twist on the classic tarte tatin. They taste just as good and have the added benefit of being available all year round.

The orange blossom water, made from the distilled spring flowers of the Seville orange, is used in many Persian sweets, teas, and jams, and goes so well with the apricots. You can find it in the baking aisle of most large supermarkets.

Bake the tart in a 8-inch cake pan if your frying pan doesn't go in the oven.

$^3/_4$ cup soft brown sugar
2 tbsp cold water
2 $^1/_2$ tbsp unsalted butter
$^1/_2$ tsp ground cinnamon
$^1/_2$ tsp vanilla extract
1 x 15-oz can of apricot halves in fruit juice, drained
All-purpose flour, for dusting
1 x $^3/_4$-lb sheet of ready-rolled puff pastry

2 tsp sliced pistachios (or roughly chopped pistachios)

For the orange blossom cream:
$^1/_2$ cup mascarpone
$^1/_2$ tsp orange blossom water
1 tsp orange zest
1 tsp lemon juice
2 tsp confectioners' sugar

Put the sugar and water into a 8-inch heavy-based ovenproof frying pan and cook over a medium heat until the sugar begins to caramelize. Remove from the heat and stir in the butter, cinnamon, and vanilla extract.

Keep stirring the caramel for a few minutes until the butter is fully combined, then remove from the heat and arrange the apricot halves in the pan, cut side up; bear in mind that the caramel will still be hot. Set aside for 10 minutes, so the apricots can absorb the flavors.

Pre-heat the oven to 375°F. Lightly dust your work surface with some flour and then roll out your pastry to $^1/_8$ inch thick. Place a dinner plate on top of the pastry, and then cut around it. Place this disc on top of the fruit in your frying pan and tuck in the edges around the fruit. If you are using a cake pan to bake the tart, transfer the fruit to this first and put the pastry on top, remembering to tuck in the edges.

Prick the surface of the pastry a few times with a fork and then place the tart in the oven and bake for 25–30 minutes until the pastry is golden brown and crisp on top.

Meanwhile, prepare your cream by combining the mascarpone with the orange blossom water, orange zest, lemon juice, and sugar.

Lightly toast the pistachios in a small pan over a low heat for a minute or two and then set aside.

When the tart is ready, remove from the oven and place a large plate over the pan. With oven gloves on, quickly and decisively invert the tart onto your plate. You need to be very strong and steady with your hands to avoid hot caramel spilling.

Leave the tart to cool for a few minutes to allow the caramel to set. Serve warm with a sprinkling of pistachios on top and a dollop of orange blossom cream on the side of each serving.

Serves 4

Orange blossom
and date pudding
Ferni

*This quick, elegant pudding is
loved all over the Middle East,
where it is flavored with rose
water, cardamom, cloves, date
syrup, figs, or mulberries, in
various combinations. One
year when my grandmother
came to visit us from Iran,
my sister Maryam casually
mentioned to her that she liked
it a lot. My gran then proceeded
to cook ferni for her every day
for the next two weeks. It says
a lot about how good it tastes
that we never got sick of it.*

*The recipe is supremely
flexible and is just as good
with almond, soy, or coconut
milk if you are avoiding dairy.
It can be served warm or cold,
depending on the season and
your preference.*

$^3/_4$ cup ground rice
  (see page 24)
4 cups whole milk
$^1/_2$ cup sugar
2 tsp orange blossom water
1 tbsp chopped pistachios,
  to decorate

For the date syrup:
2 tbsp honey
3 tbsp water
$^1/_8$ tsp ground cinnamon
$^1/_4$ cup Iranian or Medjool dates,
  pitted and roughly chopped
2 tsp orange blossom water

Mix the ground rice and 1 cup of the milk together until they form a
smooth paste.

Pour the rest of the milk and the sugar into a large saucepan over a medium
heat and slowly whisk the rice mixture into it. Cook for 15 minutes, stirring
frequently, to stop it catching on the base of the pan.

Add the orange blossom water and cook for another 2 minutes. Take off the
heat and pour into a large serving dish (around 9 inches wide) or six
individual glasses or ramekins. Leave to set for 10 minutes.

Make the syrup by cooking the honey, water, cinnamon, orange blossom
water, and dates in a small saucepan over a medium heat for 3–4 minutes
until the dates have softened.

Toast the pistachios in a small pan over a medium heat for a minute or two.

Just before serving, drizzle some date syrup over the puddings (adjusting the
amount to suit your sweet tooth) and finish with the pistachios.

Serves 6

Cardamom crème caramel

Iranians have a soft spot for a French dessert and this is one of the classics: a retro fix that continues to wobble its way on to dinner tables and restaurant menus across the country. This recipe introduces sweet and warming cardamom to the custard; I also like to add a few dried rose petals, crumbled on top of the caramel, for a floral flourish, though these are not strictly essential. I love serving the crème caramel in individual ramekins but if you prefer, you can make it in a large dish and bake for about an hour, until the whole surface of the pudding is firm to the touch.

Unsalted butter, for greasing
8 cardamom pods
Scant cup whole milk
1 cup + 2 tbsp light cream
4 medium eggs
2 tbsp superfine sugar
1 tsp vanilla extract

For the caramel:
$^1/_2$ cup superfine sugar
4 tbsp hot water

To finish (optional):
Dried rose petals

Grease six medium-sized ramekins with a little butter and set aside.

For the caramel, put the sugar in a saucepan, cover with the water, and gently cook over a low heat until the sugar forms a thick, dark syrup. (To check if it is done, pour a little from a teaspoon into a glass of cold water. If it sets, it is ready.) Working quickly, before it sets, divide the caramel evenly among your ramekins, swirling to cover the bases.

Pre-heat your oven to 300°F and then start making the custard.

Place the cardamom pods in a mortar and work with a pestle to get the seeds out. Discard the pods and grind the seeds to a fine powder.

Pour the milk, cream, and ground cardamom into the pan you used to make your caramel. Slowly bring to a simmer over a low heat, using a whisk to melt any bits of caramel from the pan into the milk. As soon as the milk starts to boil, take it off the heat and leave to cool for at least 5 minutes.

Crack the eggs into a large bowl and beat in the sugar. Slowly, one ladle at a time, pour the milk into the eggs, whisking as you go to prevent the eggs from curdling. Add the vanilla extract. Strain the custard through a sieve to remove any curdled bits of egg then pour into your ramekins.

Place the ramekins in a large roasting pan and then add enough boiling water to come halfway up the sides of the moulds. Bake in the oven for 25–30 minutes, until the custard is set and the whole surface is firm to the touch.

When the crème caramels are ready, leave to cool and then chill in the fridge for at least 3 hours.

Just before serving, run a butter knife around the insides of the ramekins, then place a serving plate on top of each one and swiftly turn out the crème caramel. If you like, finish with a pinch of dried rose petals.

Serves 6

Saffron, rose water, and pistachio ice cream
Bastani sonnati

Ice cream parlors light up the streets of Iranian cities at night, and in the summer months groups of young people and families gather around the rickety old plastic tables outside, sampling a bountiful array of colorful frozen creams and sorbets. This is the recipe for Iran's most famous ice cream, a saffron and rose water infused custard, dotted with toasted pistachios. It is served in a number of ways in Iran—plain or sandwiched between two ice-cream wafers or scooped into a glass of fresh carrot juice (a personal favorite).

½ tsp saffron strands
A pinch of sugar
2 tbsp freshly boiled water
1½ tbsp chopped pistachios
1 cup whole milk

6 egg yolks
⅔ cup superfine sugar
Scant cup heavy cream
1½ tsp rose water
1 tbsp dried rose petals (optional)

Make a saffron liquid by grinding the saffron strands with a pinch of sugar in a pestle and mortar and then adding the boiled water. Leave to steep.

Lightly toast the pistachios in a small pan over a low heat for a minute or two. Set aside to cool.

Gently heat the milk in a saucepan until it starts to steam. Take it off the heat before it comes to the boil and set aside.

Whisk the egg yolks and the sugar together until the eggs have doubled in size and are paler in color.

Slowly, in three or four batches, pour the hot milk into the eggs, whisking all the time to make sure the mixture doesn't curdle. Pour into a large saucepan and cook over a very low heat for about 8 minutes until the custard has thickened, gently stirring the whole time to prevent curdling.

When the custard is nice and thick, take it off the heat and stir through the saffron liquid and rose water. Strain through a sieve into a mixing bowl to catch any curdled bits of egg, then leave to cool to room temperature. Whisk the cream through the custard and place in the fridge to chill for 30 minutes.

Spoon the mixture into an ice cream maker and churn according to the manufacturer's instructions, adding the pistachios halfway through the process. Transfer to a plastic container and freeze for at least 2 hours.

When ready to serve, remove from the freezer for 5 minutes or until slightly softened, and sprinkle with dried rose petals, if you like.

Serves 4–6

Choux buns with rose water and pistachio cream
Naan-e khame-i

These light-as-air buns are a quintessential Iranian dessert, a sweet, year-round treat that everybody loves. Making choux pastry is surprisingly quick and easy but you do need to follow the instructions carefully. To prevent the buns from going soggy in the middle, be sure to beat the flour, water, and butter well during the initial cooking over the stovetop. And when the saucepan goes back on the heat, it is crucial to keep stirring the mixture, to ensure that your dough rises properly.

The cream filling can make the buns go soggy if added too soon, so it's best to do this just before serving. You can flavor the filling with orange blossom water or vanilla extract in place of the rose water—they all taste delicious.

For the pastry:
2 oz (¹/₂ stick) unsalted butter, cubed, plus extra for greasing
¹/₂ cup water
¹/₂ cup + 1 tbsp white bread flour
A pinch of fine sea salt
1 tsp superfine sugar
2 medium eggs, beaten

For the egg wash:
1 medium egg, beaten

For the filling:
³/₄ cup heavy cream
¹/₄ cup confectioners' sugar, for dusting
1 tsp rose water
1¹/₂ tbsp shelled, unsalted pistachios

Pre-heat the oven to 400°F. Line a baking tray with parchment paper and lightly grease with butter.

Bring the water to the boil in a saucepan over a low heat, adding the butter to let it melt. As soon as the water begins to boil, take the saucepan off the heat, tip in the flour, salt, and sugar and beat vigorously for a minute. Place the saucepan back on the heat and cook for 2 minutes, stirring the mixture continuously with a wooden spoon. Remove the saucepan from the heat and leave the mixture to cool for a few minutes. Mix in the 2 beaten eggs, a little at a time, until the dough is smooth, glossy, and fairly stiff. This should take around 3–4 minutes.

Spoon tablespoonfuls of dough onto the baking tray until all the dough is used up and you have 12 roughly equal-sized balls. Using a pastry brush, smooth down the tops of the buns with the egg wash, getting rid of any knobbly bits. Bake in the pre-heated oven for 15 minutes, then turn the temperature down to 325°F for about 10–15 minutes until the buns are puffed up and golden brown on top.

Meanwhile, whisk the cream, sugar, and rose water together until medium peaks form, then set aside in the fridge.

Remove one bun from the oven and tear it apart to see if it is cooked all the way through. Then remove all the pastries from the oven, pierce the tops with a fork to let some steam out, and leave to cool completely on a rack.

Just before serving, toast the pistachios in a small pan and then grind them to coarse crumbs with a pestle and mortar. Put aside 1 teaspoon of the ground pistachios. Fold the rest into the chilled rose-water cream.

Place the cream in a piping bag and make a small incision with a knife into the side of each bun. Carefully squeeze each bun full of cream till it puffs up. Alternatively, slice the puffs in half and use a teaspoon to fill them with cream. Dust with a little confectioners' sugar and sprinkle over the ground pistachios.

Makes 12 buns

Sour cherry and dark chocolate cookies

Rich and decadent, the recipe for these luxurious cookies was the result of a visit to Café Ilio, an artisan chocolatier in northern Tehran, run by husband and wife team Sahar Hossein-Najari and Mehrdad Aghameeri. The pair spent six years traveling around Belgium, France, and Italy, honing their craft, before introducing Iranians to the wonders of fine chocolate, incorporating traditional ingredients—like saffron, pistachio, and cardamom— into a whole new world of truffles, macaroons, jams, and cakes. Thanks to their winning combination of dark chocolate and sour cherries, these cookies are loved by adults and children alike.

1¼ cups all-purpose flour
¼ cocoa powder
½ tsp baking soda
½ tsp baking powder
¼ tsp fine sea salt
5 oz (1¼ sticks) unsalted butter
½ cup soft dark brown sugar
¼ cup + 2 tbsp granulated sugar

1 large egg
1 tsp vanilla extract
½ cup dark chocolate chips
¾ cup sour cherries (or regular dried cherries), roughly chopped
Flaky sea salt, for sprinkling (optional)

Place the flour, cocoa powder, baking soda, baking powder, and salt in a bowl.

In an electric mixer with a beater attachment, or in a bowl with a wooden spoon, cream the butter and both sugars together until light and fluffy. Add the egg and vanilla extract, then gradually beat in the cocoa-flour mixture. Stir in the dark chocolate chips and sour cherries, then cover the bowl with plastic wrap and place in the fridge for an hour (up to 2 days).

Pre-heat the oven to 325°F. Line two baking sheets with parchment paper.

When the dough is firm, take it out of the fridge and roll it into 12 balls about the size of a golf ball—about 2 inches round, 2 oz in weight (an ice cream scoop is ideal for measuring the balls out). Place the balls on the baking trays, making sure you leave plenty of room (about ½-inch) between them, as they will spread out a lot (don't be tempted to pat them down).

Bake the cookies for around 14–18 minutes. They are ready when a fork stuck into the middle of a cookie comes out clean. If you are baking the cookies on different shelves in the oven they will cook at different speeds so you may have to take one batch out earlier than the other; keep a close eye on them.

Leave the cookies to cool for 5 minutes on the trays, as they will be too fragile to move straight away, then transfer to a wire rack to cool completely. I like to sprinkle mine with a little sea salt at this stage to offset the sweetness of the chocolate, but that is entirely optional.

Makes 12 large cookies

Date and walnut squares no

In the spring and summer months, Iranians flock to the high mountains and green forests of the Caspian littoral for their holidays and many return with packets of "koloocheh," a date and walnut filled pastry from the town of Fuman in Gilan. This recipe is a trip down memory lane for me, as it transports all the key ingredients of those sweet parcels into simple oat-crumble squares. They make a good snack to take on hikes or picnics, and are incredibly moreish with a cup of tea in the afternoon. To make them vegan, simply replace the butter with the same amount of virgin coconut oil.

$3/4$ cup walnuts
4 cardamom pods
Scant cup Iranian or Medjool
  dates, pitted and roughly chopped
4 cloves, ground
$1/2$ tsp ground cinnamon
$3/4$ cup water

$1^1/_2$ cups all-purpose flour
1 cup old-fashioned rolled oats
$3/4$ cup brown sugar
$1/2$ tsp baking powder
A pinch of fine sea salt
6 oz ($1^1/_2$ sticks) unsalted butter, cubed, plus extra for greasing

Grind the walnuts to a fine powder with a pestle and mortar, spice grinder, or food processor.

Place the cardamom pods in a mortar and work with a pestle to get the seeds out of the pods. Discard the pods and grind the seeds to a fine powder. Place the dates, ground cardamom, cloves, cinnamon, and water in a small saucepan. Bring to the boil and then reduce the heat and simmer for about 8–10 minutes until the mixture is a smooth and thick paste. Take off the heat, add the ground walnuts and leave to cool.

Pre-heat your oven to 350°F. Grease an 8-inch square baking pan and line it with parchment paper.

Put the flour, oats, sugar, baking powder, and a generous pinch of salt in a large mixing bowl. Add the butter and combine with your fingers until you get a crumble mixture.

Press half of the oat mixture onto the bottom of the cake pan and press down firmly. Spoon the date and walnut paste evenly on top, pressing down lightly with the back of your spoon to evenly distribute it. Top with the remaining oats and lightly press down.

Bake for 45 minutes or until the oat topping is golden. Allow to cool and then cut into squares.

Makes around 24 squares

Planning a meal

Persian food doesn't separate starters from main courses; instead small dishes are interspersed with larger ones on the dining table and guests simply help themselves to as little or as much of each dish as they fancy. Natural yogurt, either plain or mixed with some vegetables, and a crisp salad or platter of fresh herbs are also present at every Persian meal and are necessary to bring some lightness, freshness, crunch, and tang to complement the earthy, rich flavors of the stews and rice dishes.

Iranian New Year

Mixed herb kuku, page 72
Mixed herb rice with baked salmon, page 158
Salad Shirazi, page 88

Choux buns with rose water and pistachio cream, page 214

Vegetarian feast

Eggplant and mushroom tahcheen, page 142
Yogurt with spinach and garlic, page 65
Carrot and pistachio salad, page 96

Rhubarb and cardamom cheesecake, page 204

Vegan feast

Eggplant fesenjoon, page 170
Persian rice (replace butter with sunflower oil), page 136
Salad Shirazi, page 88

Orange blossom and date pudding (use non-dairy milk), page 210

Barbecue

Corn with sumac and za'atar-spiced butter, page 71
Persian rice, page 136
Dr. Asaf's juicy lamb kebabs, page 182
Lime and saffron chicken kebabs, page 164
Yogurt with pomegranate and mint, page 65
Mixed herb platter, page 54

Persian picnic
Saffron, potato, and barberry kuku, page 76
Cucumber salad with sekanjibeen dressing, page 90
Fava bean, sour cherry, and rice salad, page 105

Date and walnut squares, page 218

Christmas or Thanksgiving
Pistachio soup, page 126

Roast chicken with pomegranate and za'atar glaze, page 175
Red cabbage, beet, and date salad, page 99
Persian rice, page 136

Poached quince with mascarpone and pistachios, page 206

Quick and easy weekday suppers
Spicy lentil and tamarind soup, page 119
Butternut squash and dried lime soup, page 122
Chicken livers with pomegranate molasses, page 68
Garlicky beans with dill and egg, page 151
Spiced beef with eggs and spring onions, page 186
Bandari fishcakes with a tamarind and date sauce, page 155
Grilled mackerel with a spicy pomegranate salsa, page 156
Herby baked falafels with a fennel and watercress salad, page 79

List of gluten-free recipes

List of dairy-free recipes

Index

About the author

Yasmin Khan is a writer and cook from London who loves to share people's stories through food. An avid traveler whose passport is never too far from her pocket, she runs cooking classes, pop-up supper clubs, and writing retreats around the world. Prior to immersing herself in the fragrances and flavors of the Persian kitchen, Yasmin worked as a human rights campaigner, running national and international campaigns for nonprofits and grassroots groups, with a special focus on the Middle East.

thesaffrontales.com   *@yasmin_khan*

About the photographers

Shahrzad Darafsheh is a Tehran-based photographer specializing in narrative, documentary, fine art, and portrait photography. She is inspired by nature and capturing the intimate spaces of reality forged between people and places.

shahrzaddarafsheh.com

Matt Russell is a London-based photographer specializing in food, travel, lifestyle, and portraiture. With a strong reputation for his natural style and ability to capture life, Matt has established himself internationally as a trusted, reputable photographer.

mattrussell.co.uk

Acknowledgments

This project wouldn't have been possible without the 277 people from across the globe who backed my Kickstarter in 2013. Thank you for taking a chance on my dream.

Thanks to James O'Nions for first suggesting I write a book about Persian food and Mel Tompkins for encouraging me to give it a go, all those years back, on a plane to Thailand.

Thanks to all of the Iranians who feature in this book and the many more who didn't make the final edition but who opened their homes so generously to me. I am humbled by your warmth and hospitality, and touched by your deep desire to show the world the real Iran.

To Shahrzad Darafsheh for her incredible location shots, adventurous spirit, and friendship—I couldn't have wished for a better partner on this project.

To my wonderful agent, Clare Hulton, for her passion, enthusiasm, and support.

To Alison Cowan, Natalie Bellos, Xa Shaw Stewart, and Zelda Turner for helping me craft the best possible version of the book. To Marina Asenjo, Tess Viljoen, Ellen Williams, and Lena Hall at Bloomsbury. To Catherine Phipps for helping finesse the recipes and Sarah Greeno for her beautiful design. To Matt Russell, Rosie Reynolds, and Tamzin Fernando for making all the food look so delicious.

To Daiee Cyrus, Ali Alipour, and Ahmad Alipour for their assistance with the research trips in Iran. To Pedar Bozorg, Madar Bozorg, Daiee Abbas, Zan Daiee Roya, Siamak, Babak, Daiee Mohammad, Zan Daiee Fariba, Amir-Hassan, Ariana, Daiee Vahid, Zan Daiee Mojgan, Sam, Sepantah, Khaleh Tahereh, Hassan Agha, Sara, Reza Esfandi, Sahand and Khaleh Tamineh for always making Astaneh feel like home.

To all my friends from the Bay for being an intrinsic part of this story. To Yinka Latevi Tuakli and Glynn Ryland, my biggest fans and most trusted mentors, thanks for always having faith.

To Kasia Kmiecik, Louise De Villiers, Mike Podmore, Olga Rodrigues, Natascha Mueller-Hirth, Adam Doran, Alistair Alexander, Gemma Houldey, Max Watson, Gail Cameron, Sheila Menon, Natasha Moskovici, Faith Louise-Hill, and Alice Holly Field for all their recipe-testing, recipe-eating, and longstanding moral support.

To Randall, who supported me throughout the process of writing this book with more love, patience, and encouragement than I could have hoped for.

To Dad and Maryam—my most trusted food critics—for their unwavering support through thick and thin, and their unbridled enthusiasm.

And finally to Maman, my inspiration and my rock, without whom none of this would have been possible.

List of Kickstarter backers

A King ❋ AA ❋ AL Kennedy ❋ Abhiyana Dhara ❋ Adam ❋ Adib Nessim ❋ Adrian Cromar ❋ Ahmad Ali Yavari ❋ Ahmad Fathjalali ❋ Aimee Matthew-John ❋ Akram ❋ Aldo Mussi ❋ Alex Pilcher ❋ Alex Rees ❋ Alexander Kravitz ❋ Ali Amani ❋ Ali Fathe Jalali ❋ Alipours ❋ Alistair ❋ Amy Potter ❋ Aneta Jedrzejewska ❋ Angella Okawa ❋ Anna ❋ Anna Smith ❋ Anne Crerar ❋ Anne Heaton ❋ Anne Sheedy ❋ Antony Loizou ❋ Arshad Mahmood ❋ Asad Rehman ❋ Asaf Khan ❋ Ashkon Jafari ❋ Audrey Mcelravy ❋ Babak Bahamin ❋ Mrs Banba Dawson ❋ Baran Dokht ❋ Barney ❋ Ben Jackman ❋ Behi Ayers ❋ Ben Hayes ❋ Bob Zomer ❋ Bradley Copping ❋ Brian Lane Lewis ❋ Brian Robert Dunaway ❋ Carlos Grijalva ❋ Carry Kim ❋ Catherine Geissler ❋ Catherine Hayes ❋ Cathy Pearson ❋ Charmian Beer ❋ Chouf ❋ Cilius Victor ❋ Clare Harvey ❋ Clare Solomon ❋ Daniel ❋ Daniel Kidd ❋ Daniella Jaeger ❋ Danielle Trafton ❋ Daryoush Jafari ❋ Dave Randall ❋ Dave Tucker ❋ David Madole ❋ David Todman ❋ Debbie Quargnolo ❋ Deborah Coles ❋ Dede Watkins ❋ Delor ❋ Dena Bugel-Shunra ❋ Denise Ajiri ❋ Douglas Mailly ❋ Dylan Howitt ❋ Dylan Satow ❋ Ed O ❋ Edward McCarthy & Lizzie Coker ❋ Elaine Gibbs ❋ Elena Brower & Erica Jago ❋ Eliot Beer ❋ Eliza Prévost ❋ Elizabeth Withers ❋ Elke Parsa ❋ Emma Dwyer ❋ Erika Podmore ❋ Estelle du Boulay ❋ Ewa Jasiewicz ❋ Fahim Rochford ❋ Faramarz ❋ Farhad Nadjm ❋ Farid Heydari ❋ Fatemeh Miri ❋ Fatemeh Rabiee Khan ❋ Faten Zaghloul ❋ Florence Rose Llewellyn ❋ GAH ❋ Gemma Houldey ❋ Geoffrey Ward ❋ Geometrical Inc. & Rambod Radmard ❋ Ghazaleh ❋ Ghobad Heidari ❋ Giedre Paludne ❋ Gillian Beddows ❋ Glynn Ryland ❋ Graeme Morrison ❋ Greg Muttitt ❋ Guy Meredith ❋ HP Albarelli ❋ Harry ❋ Helen Rosser ❋ Helen Shaw ❋ Homa Daryaei ❋ Hora Ejtehadi ❋ Hosanna Fox ❋ James Haywood ❋ James O'Nions ❋ Janna Moore ❋ Jasmine ❋ Jean Bacon ❋ Jess Phillips ❋ Jess Southwood ❋ Jess Tyrrell ❋ Jessica Beck ❋ Jessica McKenzie Mason ❋ Jethro Soutar ❋ Joanne ❋ John Hilary ❋ John Hughes ❋ John Rees ❋ John Rynne ❋ Josiah Halasz ❋ Joy ❋ Junaid Rathore ❋ Karen Robson ❋ Kasia Kmiecik ❋ Kat Bailey ❋ Kate Horner ❋ Kevin Bate ❋ Kevin Blowe ❋ Kirsten Berg ❋ Kirsty Wright ❋ Laura Smith ❋ Layla Auer ❋ Leigh Martens ❋ Leila Mojtahedi ❋ Liesbeth Groot Jebbink ❋ Lisa Gansky ❋ Lisa Kerrigan ❋ Liz Sasso-K ❋ Lorna Gatherer Ford ❋ Lorraine ❋ Louisa ❋ Louise de Villiers ❋ Lubna Sharief ❋ Lulu Sturdy ❋ Lynn Chaitman ❋ Mahendra Nath ❋ Malika ❋ Maria Anne Sagar ❋ Mark Olden ❋ Mark Werth ❋ Marwan Marwan ❋ Maryam khan ❋ Matt Watson ❋ Matthew London ❋ Matthew McGregor ❋ Max Watson ❋ Meg Carlson ❋ Megan Baker ❋ Megan Flamer ❋ Mehdi Heydari ❋ Mehran Fatemifar ❋ Mehri Heidari ❋ Melanie Kramers ❋ Melanie Tompkins ❋ Menonymous ❋ Michael Forlife ❋ Michael G ❋ Michael Houldey ❋ Michael Podmore ❋ Michal Rosenn ❋

Mikeysmiling ❋ Mina Mojtahedi ❋ Moberley ❋ Mohamed Al-Salem ❋ Murtaza Arif ❋ Najma ❋ NK ❋ Nader Heydari ❋ Nadia ❋ Nahid ❋ Namdar Baghaei-Yazdi ❋ Narzanin ❋ Nasim Naraghi ❋ Natalie Dendy ❋ Natalie Oppong-Wiafe ❋ Natascha Mueller-Hirth ❋ Natasha Moskovici ❋ Naz Massoumi ❋ Neil Foster ❋ Nick Alexandra ❋ Nick Griffiths ❋ Nicole Davis ❋ Nicole Hermes ❋ Nicole Primpke ❋ Nihal Rabbani ❋ Niki Hart ❋ Nina Eder-Haslehner ❋ Osman Junaid ❋ Owen Espley ❋ Paige Marie Reeves ❋ Paula Reid ❋ Peter Richard Brooks ❋ Peter Winfield ❋ Peyvand Sadeghian ❋ Poupak Bahamin ❋ Raisa Breslava ❋ Ramalingam Mohan ❋ Ramesh Ram ❋ Randall Oleary ❋ Richard Cox ❋ Roberto Bertini Renzetti ❋ Robin Layfield ❋ Ronny Nicholas ❋ Roy Two Thousand ❋ Rubina Jasani ❋ Sam Heidari ❋ Sander Enderink ❋ Sandra Mason ❋ Sara ❋ Sara Tietz Kozel ❋ Sahar Zadeh ❋ Sarah Beck ❋ Sarah Reader ❋ Sarah Sylvester ❋ Sasson Mansoori ❋ Sayed Munaf Ahmed ❋ Scarlet Granville ❋ Schirin Chams-Diba ❋ Scott Boden ❋ Sepideh Ebrahimzadeh ❋ Shahin Yazdani ❋ Shahryar Mazkoory ❋ Shannon Sailer ❋ Shawn Cathcart ❋ Sheri Rahmanian ❋ Shida Mohammadi ❋ Shirin Fatemifar ❋ Si Chan ❋ Siamak Fathe Jalali ❋ Simon Phillips ❋ Sinead Cummins ❋ Soodabehyavari ❋ Sophie Pritchard ❋ Sosen Botani ❋ Stephanie Cucchi ❋ Stephanos Pantelas ❋ Stephen Cockburn ❋ Sudha ❋ Sue Branford ❋ Sue Nyirenda ❋ Sundus & Ihab Tewfik ❋ Susanna Clark ❋ Tahmineh Smith ❋ Thomas Schulze ❋ Tom Dennison ❋ Tom Gorman ❋ Tom Mansfield ❋ Tony Katz ❋ Tony Rasmussen ❋ Torgamous ❋ Uli Kindermann ❋ Veronica Sjöberg ❋ Vicki H ❋ Victor ❋ Vikas Shepherd ❋ William J McNicoll ❋ Yasaman Shahkhalili ❋ ZuZuBe

Bloomsbury Publishing
An imprint of Bloomsbury Publishing Plc

50 Bedford Square   1385 Broadway
London   New York
WC1B 3DP   NY 10018
UK   USA

www.bloomsbury.com

First published in Great Britain 2016

Library of Congress cataloging-in-publication data is available.
A catalogue record for this book is available from the British Library.

HB ISBN: 978-1-63286-710-0
ePub ISBN: 978-1-63286-711-7

2 4 6 8 10 9 7 5 3 1

Project editor: Zelda Turner
Designer and illustrator: Sarah Greeno sarahgreeno.com
Travel photographer: Shahrzad Darafsheh
Recipe photographer: Matt Russell
Food stylist: Rosie Reynolds
Prop stylist: Tamzin Ferdinando
Indexer: Hilary Bird

Printed and bound in China by C&C Offset Printing Co. Ltd

To find out more about our authors and books visit www.bloomsbury.com. Here you will
find extracts, author interviews, details of forthcoming events and the option to sign up for
our newsletters.